Lessons in Lean Management

53 Ideas to Transform Services

LESSONS IN Lean Management

53 Ideas to Transform Services

DEBASHIS SARKAR

Westland Ltd

westland ltd

Venkat Towers, 165, P.H. Road, Maduravoyal, Chennai 600 095
No. 38/10 (New No. 5), Raghava Nagar, New Timber Yard Layout, Bangalore 560 026
Survey No. A – 9, II Floor, Moula Ali Industrial Area, Moula Ali, Hyderabad 500 040
23/181, Anand Nagar, Nehru Road, Santacruz East, Mumbai 400 055
4322/3, Ansari Road, Daryaganj, New Delhi 110 002

First published by westland ltd 2012

10 9 8 7 6 5 4 3 2 1

ISBN: 978-93-81626-80-1

Typeset by FourWords Inc.

Printed at Thomson Press (India) Ltd.

In memory of my Dad,
who left us too soon

Table of Contents

List of Figures *x*
List of Tables *xiii*
Acknowledgements *xvi*
Preface *xviii*
Note to Readers *xxi*
Introduction *xxiii*

Section 1: Philosophies

1. Lean in Services and Manufacturing: What's the Difference 3
2. Understanding Lean 7
3. The Customer will not Pay for Everything in a Process 14
4. Cost Cutting is not Lean Thinking 18
5. Adopt a Quiver Approach 24
6. Know the Fundamental Differences between the Services and Manufacturing Processes 30
7. Not Just Metrics But the Right Metrics 34
8. Begin Your Journey with a Holistic Roadmap 40
9. Power Your Lean Journey with the Art of Observation 44
10. Process Should Positively Impact the key Stakeholders 51

11. Service Guarantees Can be a Good Aspiration 55

12. Do Not Always Brand the Method of Change 60

SECTION 2: PEOPLE

13. Lean Cannot Solely be the Top Management's Agenda 66

14. Explain Why We Do What We Do 71

15. Create Interest so your Team Appreciates the Power of Lean 75

16. Encourage Teams and Individuals to Report Problems 79

17. Lean is More Than Just Tools 84

18. Employee Attrition is a Major Cause of Inefficiency 89

19. Build A Culture of Process Thinking 94

20. Resources are Wasted when Employees do not know what Service Means to Them 97

21. Continually Create a Sense of Urgency 102

22. Ensure that Middle Management is Fully Engaged 107

SECTION 3: PROCESS

23. The DEB LOREX™ Model for Lean Transformation 114

24. Lead Time and Throughput Time are not the Same 118

25. Lean should Positively Impact the Tetra-Headed Business Outcomes 124

26. Continually Ascertain the Health of Lean 129

27. Process Ownership is the Key to Enhancing Efficiency 132

28. Value-stream Management is the Heart of Lean 137

29. Create a Process Repository 140

30. Set Up a Lean Office 144

31. The Role of the Lean Office Should Change Over Time 149

32. Embed A3 Thinking 154

33. Follow A Holistic Approach to Visual Management System 161

34. Institutionalize the Process of Reflection 165

35. Institutionalize the LIP-SIP Engine for Improvements 169

SECTION 4: PROBLEM SOLVING

36. Ohno's Wastes are Applicable to Service Organizations 177

37. Inventory in a Services Context can be Quite Esoteric 181

38. Administer the Opportunity Questionnaire to Judge Lean Applicability 186

39. Make Customers Serve Themselves 190

40. Do Not Forget Waste in Functional Crevices 194

41. White Spaces can be Potential Opportunities for Lean Application 203

42. Distribute and Optimize Capacity Via Multi-Skilling 208

43. Is your Cross-Selling Inefficiently Ineffective? 214

44. Instill An Enterprise-wide Problem-solving Process 218

45. Only Focussing on a Good Service Recovery Process can be Quite Myopic 224

46. Too Many MIS Reports can make Business Ineffective 228

47. Use Sales Partners to Build Relationships 233

48. Practice Visual Management 237

49. A Little-Known Law has Huge Powers to Drive Lean Solutions 243

50. Creating A Good Pull System Can Take Time 248

51. Use Little's Law to Create Pull in Transaction Processing 252

52. Being Aware of Wastes Can Make Business Acquisition Agile, Efficient and Effective 255

53. Mindless Standardization of Processes does not Work in Services 265

Epilogue 272
Glossary 276
References 282
Index 285

List of Figures

Title

Section 1

1.1 DEB-LOREX™ Model for Lean Transformation 11
1.2 Lean and Travel Costs 21
1.3 Outcomes of Lean Over Time 43

Section 2

2.1 Process of Alignment in a Multi-location Global Conglomerate 73
2.2 Taxonomy of Resistance within Organizations 86
2.3 Adoption to Engagement: The Lean Approach 87
2.4 What's the problem? Ask the process! 96

Section 3

3.1 DEB-LOREX™ Model for Lean Transformation 115
3.2 Cause and Effect Relationship of DEB-LOREX™ Model for Lean Transformation 116
3.3 Difference between Lead Time and Throughput Time 119

3.4 Before and After Picture of a Layout Change after a Lean Event 123
3.5 The Tetra-Headed Outcomes of Lean 125
3.6 The DEB-LOREX™ Model and the Tetra-Headed Outcomes of Lean 127
3.7 Joint Ownership of Process by Senior Members of Functions 134
3.8 Members from the Leadership Team own the Process 134
3.9 Generic Value Stream 138
3.10 Value Stream of a Mortgage Finance Business 139
3.11 Structure of a Process Repository 141
3.12 Various Constituents of a Lean Office 145
3.13 Changing Complexion of the Lean Office 151
3.14 Template for A3 Problem Solving 156
3.15 A3 Template for Strategic Planning 158
3.16 A3 Template for Proposal Writing 159
3.17 Approach for Visual Management 162
3.18 Process for Reflection 166
3.19 LIP-SIP Construct of Improvements 170
3.20 Small and Large Improvement Projects in Deming's Wheel 173

SECTION 4

4.1 Pull in Cash Management Process in a Retail Branch 185
4.2 Value-Added, Non-Value-Added, Business-Value-Added Activity in Function 196
4.3 Finding White Spaces in Processes 205
4.4 Key Variables Impacting Strategic Business Objectives 206
4.5 Typical Push-based Cross-sell Process 215

4.6 New Pull-based Cross-sell Process 216
4.7 Philosophical Difference between Normal Cross-selling and Lean Cross-selling 216
4.8 The PDCA cycle 219
4.9 Toyota Business Practices 221
4.10 Role of Sales Partners in a Company instilling Lean thinking 235
4.11 Back-Office Process Shop Functions 245
4.12 Step-wise Approach to Creating a Pull System 250
4.13 Stipulated Inventory in a Credit Processing Cell 254
4.14 Process Visibility and Degree of Standardization 268
4.15 The Process Matrix 268

List of Tables

Title of Tables

Section 1

1.1 Activities and their Values 16
1.2 Activities and their Treatment under Lean 20
1.3 Problem Type and Improvement Methodology 27
1.4 Deb's A to H Principles of Metrics 35
1.5 Template for Metrics Effectiveness 37
1.6 Interpretation of Scores for Effective Metrics Management 38
1.7 Broad Roadmap of Implementation 41
1.8 Deb's 10 Rules for Workplace Observation 46
1.9 Deb's Questionnaire on Effectiveness of Process Optimization 53
1.10 To-Dos for Customer Guarantees 57

Section 2

2.1 Active and Passive Resistance 84
2.2 Challenges to Making Lean an Integral Part of Organizational Fabric 85
2.3 Approach to Service Intent Deployment 99

SECTION 3

3.1 Various Times of Lean 119
3.2 Deb's Lean Health Assessment Tool 130
3.3 Interpreting Scores from Deb's Lean Health Assessment Tool 131
3.4 Role of a Process Owner 135
3.5 Hierarchies of Process and how to make them Visible 142
3.6 The Composition of a Lean Office. 145
3.7 A Changing Central Lean Office. 152
3.8 PDCA and Problem Solving Steps 155
3.9 The Do's and Dont's of a Reflection Process 167
3.10 Examples of Large and Small Improvement Projects 171

SECTION 4

4.1 Eight Wastes of Lean (with examples) 178
4.2 Wastes Observed in Cash Projects 185
4.3 Deb's Lean Opportunity Questionnaire 187
4.4 Functional Overview Listing 195
4.5 Questions for Value-Added Activity 196
4.6 Questions for Business-Value-Added Activity 197
4.7 Template for Inventory of Activities 198
4.8 Template for Inventory of Activities (filled) 199
4.9 Template for Inefficiency Assessment 200
4.10 Assessment of Functional Redundancies 201
4.11 Template for listing Strategic Business Objectives 206
4.12 Template for Strategic Business Objectives 207
4.13 Template for Strategic Ownership Matrix 210

4.14 Example of Activity Prioritization in Multi-Skilling 210
4.15 Gradation of Skills 211
4.16 Dashboard for Tracking Multi -Skilling 212
4.17 Details of PDCA 218
4.18 PDCA and Problem Solving 220
4.19 Metrics for Service Recovery 226
4.20 MIS Report Rationalization 229
4.21 Inventorization and Analysis of MIS Reports 230
4.22 Difference between Strategic and Tactical Visual Information 238
4.23 Deb's Instrument for Assessing Visual Management Effectiveness 239
4.24 Ratings for Deb's Instrument 241
4.25 Interpretation of Scores for Deb's Instrument 241
4.26 Branch Teller 244
4.27 Mortgage Back-Office Processing 246
4.28 Inventory in a Store 246
4.29 Deb's 12 Wastes of Customer Acquisition 256
4.30 Schedule for Typical Lean Breakthrough in a Services Setup 263

ACKNOWLEDGEMENTS

A book like this is not easy to put together. It is the result of many who have supported me in my endeavours in the practice of Lean management and while writing this book. To the following, whose support made this book possible:

- K.V. Kamath and Sanjiv Kerkar for allowing me to practice many of my ideas in one of India's best known business institutions,
- CEOs and Business Leaders around me who have challenged my thoughts and made me look at things from a different perspective, solidifying my understanding of change-management,
- Lean Leaders from all over the world (in diverse places such as Detroit, Chennai, Winterthur, Stockholm, Brussels, Ann Arbor, Shanghai, Singapore, Toronto, etc) who were kind enough to open the doors of their company and share their trials and tribulations,
- My team members in my workplace, whom I am not naming to avoid missing anybody, who worked with me tirelessly to give life to my ideas,
- Shalini Krishan, editor at Westland, for bearing with my fastidious self and embellishing the book with her language skills,

- Thought leaders, whose work is listed in detail at the end of the book, who have helped me to expand my horizon on the subject.
- My mom, Malabika, and wife, Sudeshna, for always being supportive of my authorial passion,
- My daughter, Trisha, for coming up with innocuous questions which always reinforced that there is so much to learn from children, and for bearing with my selfish pursuits which could otherwise have been time spent with her.

PREFACE

Lean management as a philosophy has existed across cultures for centuries. Its application in business, though relatively recent, is much applauded. Thanks to the work done at Toyota, we now have a practice which is being adopted by companies globally to drive operational excellence. Lean as a philosophy is so holistic in nature that it can positively impact a wide range of strategic issues such as cost, revenue, product development, employee engagement, risk management, employee productivity and customer convenience.

We know enough about the successful implementation of Lean in manufacturing companies. However, I have yet to see a company which primarily provides services that can truly be called a Lean organization. Their success at best is partial. This is mainly because these companies are somehow not aware of what it takes to implement and drive Lean in the organization.

Over the last decade I have focused on using Lean as an approach to enhance organizational performance, in order to see how it can be adopted to businesses outside the manufacturing sector, in areas beyond the production shop-floor. This has resulted in a desire to share some of my observations and experiences with Lean management in the service sector, as these can be readily adopted by organizations. The details of some of this work are encapsulated in my earlier books: *5S for Service Organizations and Offices: A Lean at Improvements* (ASQ Press, USA; 2006) and *Lean for Service Organizations and Offices: A Holistic Approach for Achieving Operational Excellence* (ASQ Press, USA; 2008). However, my friends from all over the world have been telling me to put together a book to capture these experiences in such a way that even those who are still uninitiated in Lean management will be interested in its philosophy and positive impact on their businesses. *Lessons in Lean Management: 53 Ideas to Transform Services* is an answer to this request. This book has ideas which will complement the existing cache of knowledge on Lean for the service sector. It intends to make the knowledge and experience of years of work on service Lean accessible, easy to comprehend and jargon free. Why?

Because Lean is not an idea to be adopted by those who watch quality alone; it's a way of thinking that needs to be internalized. This book is targeted to those who work in or are related to the services world and wish to understand how Lean can impact their work and productivity. I believe this book will be particularly handy to leaders as companies emerge from the current economic downturn.

The book contains a selection of important ideas which have been gathered while catalyzing operational excellence transformation using the principles of Lean management. The ideas cover a wide range of functions such as product development, sales, collections, technology, customer service, credit, human resources and so on.

This book is meant for everyone from chief executives, business leaders, Lean practitioners, Lean mavens, and Lean navigators to functional heads. It provides a glimpse of the basic principles, potential and possibilities of Lean in the service sector. For a CEO, the book provides the dos and don'ts that need to be kept in mind while leading an enterprise-wide change through Lean. For a Lean practitioner, the book provides the unique tools and techniques for Lean implementation in the service sector. They have not been published before, and I believe agents for Lean management will find them useful. But for those who are looking for just an introduction to Lean, the book provides a glimpse of what Lean is and what it takes to drive a Lean transformation. Though the lessons are primarily meant for service companies, their universal nature can also be applied to manufacturing organizations.

I look forward to your feedback on this book. Do share with me your experiences in adopting Lean as an engine for business improvement. My email id is debashissarkar4@yahoo.com

DEBASHIS SARKAR
May 2012

NOTE TO READERS

Some terms might be unfamiliar to readers:

- The DEB-LOREX™ Model stands for Deb's Lean Organizational Excellence Model, which has been created by the author to facilitate Lean transformation in service organizations. The term DEB-LOREX™ Model is a trademark owned by the author. (Deb is short for the author's first name, Debashis).
- The author has applied for trademark of the words LIP-SIP Construct of Improvements and Lean Maven.

The following tools created by the author are appearing for the first time in this book:

- Deb's A to H principles of metrics.
- Deb's 10 rules for workplace observation.
- Deb's questionnaire to determine effectiveness of process optimization/design.
- Deb's Lean heath assessment tool.
- Deb's Lean opportunity questionnaire.
- Deb's instrument for assessing visual management effectiveness.
- Deb's 12 wastes of customer-acquisition.

The words 'product' and 'service' are used synomymously in the book.

A Glossary is provided at the end of the book to demystify the technical terms used.

The term s/he is used to refer to 'she or he'.

Introduction

Lean is a management approach that endeavours to create a profitable and agile business by relentlessly focusing on what is of 'value' to the customer. It is a philosophy that not only makes your business profitable but also provides you with an engine for continual improvement.

The adoption of Lean by the service sector has been quite slow, by and large. The recent financial crisis provides an excellent context for service companies to introspect and examine the enormous potential that Lean as an approach holds for performance enhancement. A simple task would be to examine the P&L (profit and loss) of service companies across the board. It will not be difficult to determine that Lean has the ability to impact most of the line items. Beyond the P&L, it has the ability to create a nimble and agile organization prepared to tackle most business challenges. Lean as a philosophy tacitly makes a positive impact on employees and all other stakeholders which include customers, communities, partners etc.

All this however is largely a theoretical discussion until Lean is driven as a business strategy and not another improvement methodology.

So, if you head or manage a services organization what can Lean do for you as a business strategy?

Having studied a large number of companies and been a part of many transformations, I believe Lean has some great advantages. Here are some basic points:

- **Quick:** Delivers results more quickly than most other business strategies.
- **Low Investment:** Requires little investment but delivers relatively higher returns.
- **Active:** Has a bias towards action rather than theory.
- **Team Oriented:** Results happen with team participation. It is not something that can be initiated or adopted by a niche group.
- **Inclusive:** Involves employees across hierarchies.
- **Easy to Understand:** No difficult statistical tools are required.
- **Aware:** Creates heightened awareness about customers, processes and community.
- **Thorough:** Teaches you how to look for hidden inefficiencies in workplaces.

Over the years, I have maintained a diary which captures all that I have learnt, observed and un-learnt from Lean management. I have played the twin roles of observer and practitioner. This book is a result of insights that have emerged from both these roles.

The objective of this book is not to make you a master of Lean management (a few lessons can't) but provide a brief look into what a journey of Lean thinking would involve. Some of these ideas may seem apparent and others unusual but they are all critical to Lean thinking and planning. For the amateur, this book will serve as a non-technical introduction to adopting this philosophy for doing business. The book also contains tools/techniques that have been developed and successfully used by me. They are the first of their kind in the Lean world. The examples I have used in the book provide real life experiences of Lean application and can help in performance improvement.

The book has been divided into four important sections:

- **Philosophies**
- **People**
- **Process**
- **Problem Solving**

Each of these sections has lessons which are independent from each other. They are meant for a busy executive who can read one lesson at a time and take time to assimilate the learnings. My suggestion is that you go through each lesson, highlight the key points and then come back to revisit them.

The book is interspaced with boxes titled **Key Takeaways** and **From the Trenches**. Key Takeaway boxes provide summaries of each lesson. From the Trenches boxes contain real life examples of Lean adoption.

Section 1

Philosophies

PHILOSOPHIES

Philosophies refer to the underlying principles that create the science and art of Lean management. These are guiding rules that weave the wisdom of Lean knowledge for subsequent application, the theories behind the visible results. These philosophies bring clarity and ensure that leaders do not lose objectivity. Understanding the guiding principles is imperative before embarking on a Lean transformation. When teams are told why they are doing what they are doing, it ensures much better engagement.

One needs to keep in mind what the larger purpose of the company is. What does it stand for? What does it value? Toyota's purpose, for example, includes 'long-term commitment to society' and to 'company economic performance and growth'. The key essence here is to focus on the long-term benefits and avoid short-term gains which could damage the heritage and future prospects of the company. Remember, Lean management, in general, is about long-term benefits for the company.

In this section we will look at an assorted set of lessons which cover the underlying principles that govern the implementation of Lean thinking in a company.

Lesson 1

LEAN IN SERVICES AND MANUFACTURING: WHAT'S THE DIFFERENCE?

In the manufacturing world, Lean has been defined in various ways. According to *Lean Lexicon: A Graphical Glossary for Lean Thinkers*, Lean is 'a business system for organizing and managing product development, operations, suppliers, and customer relations that requires less capital, and less time to make products with fewer defects to precise customer desires, compared with the previous system of mass production.'

Since its application began in manufacturing, many people view Lean as a purely manufacturing business philosophy. They could not be more incorrect. It is essentially a way of thinking about what you produce or provide to your customer and how you can do it more efficiently, at lower cost and more profitably. While the underlying philosophy and principles remain the same in a services context, Lean could be defined as follows:

Strategic Definition of Lean for a Service Context

Lean is a management philosophy that endeavours to improve the performance of an organization by focusing on elements that do not add value. The focus is on the organization viewed holistically as a business-system that comprises elements (such as leadership, strategy, people, process, partners, value-streams, policy, structure and similar components) and makes them work in sync to deliver organizational objectives. Adoption of Lean principles should make an organization effective, efficient and adaptable; it should be able to deliver services to the customers when they need them, at a desired price, and with the expected service experience.

Tactical Definition of Lean for a Service Context

Lean is a process optimization methodology that focuses on improving the effectiveness and efficiency of a process by eliminating activities that do not add value to the customers and the product.

At a strategic level, a Lean implementation in a service context should ideally result in:

- better customer experience,
- enhanced revenue,
- reduction in cost,
- reduction in rework and rejects,
- reduction in business complexities,

- added simplifications,
- improvement in productivity,
- reduced cost of business acquisition,
- better people engagement,
- reduced operational risk,
- profitability enhancement,
- better customer loyalty.

The truth is that most managers are unable to impact even four of the above areas. This is primarily because systems, like people, get used to a certain way of functioning. We forget to constantly evaluate them to understand if they are working for the organization and the customer or not. Lean helps us focus on these issues and evaluate our present systems to streamline them for increased efficiency.

At a tactical level, the implementation of Lean to a process will result in the following:

- reduction in cycle time (time taken to complete a business activity),
- reduction in waiting time,
- reduction in query time (time taken to resolve a query),
- reduction in lead time (customer to customer time),
- reduction in throughput time (time to complete the entire process),
- reduction in defect levels,
- flawless processing of goods or services.

How this works in services is something we will discuss in subsequent lessons.

Key Takeaways

- Lean is more than a definition, it is a philosophy.
- Lean is just not about tools and techniques and it is also about people.
- Lean is looking at the organization from both the strategic and tactical lenses.
- Lean can be successfully applied to service companies but with some modifications and customization.

Lesson 2

UNDERSTANDING LEAN

While many think, and rightly so, that the concept of Lean emerged from the Toyota stable, the term Lean as we know it today was coined by John Krafcik in 1988 when he worked with James P. Womack, as a graduate student on the International Motor Vehicle Program at the Sloan School, MIT. However, the phrase 'Lean manufacturing' really became popular after the success of the bestselling book *The Machine That Changed the World* (1990) written by James P. Womack, Daniel Jones and Daniel Roos. The system suggested by them used less of everything compared to earlier mass production systems. The manufacturing space, investment in tools and the engineering hours were literally halved to develop a new product – hence, it was 'Lean'.

Lean owes its popularity to the research done by stalwarts such as James Womack, Daniel Jones, Jeffrey Liker, and John Shook, among others. Each of these thought leaders have contributed to our collective knowledge of Lean. It is, however, extremely important to understand how these principles were derived by each of them.

James Womack and Daniel Jones

In their book *Lean Thinking: Banish Wastes and Create Wealth In Your Corporation* (1996), they encapsulated the broad principles of Lean thinking and production as follows:

- Specify value from the standpoint of customer,
- Identify the value stream for the product family,
- Introduce flow: Arrange steps in tight sequence,
- Let the customer pull value from the next upstream activity,
- Endeavour to create perfection.

These may seem purely production ideas, but were the basis of further development in Lean thinking as becomes apparent in their work later. Their book *Lean Consumption: How Producers and Consumers Save Time to Create Wealth Together* (2005), talks about applying Lean principles beyond production to the consumption and provision processes. Womack and Jones proposed the following principles for Lean consumption, that every organisation providing goods or services should consider:

- Solve the customer's problem completely,
- Don't waste the customer's time,

- Provide exactly what the customer wants,
- Deliver value where the customer wants it,
- Supply value when customers want it,
- Reduce the number of decisions customers must make to solve the problem.

It is important to reflect on this transition. The ideas put forward by Womack and Jones represent a broadened understanding of the principles of Lean. The consumption principles seem to be ideally suited for services, as we shall see later.

Jeffrey Liker

In his book *The Toyota Way* (2004), Jeffrey Liker summarized the fourteen principles which are an integral part of the Toyota Motor Company. These are:

1. Base your management decisions on a long-term philosophy, even at the expense of short-term financial goals.
2. Create a continuous process flow to bring problems to the surface.
3. Use 'pull' systems to avoid overproduction.
4. Level out the workload.
5. Build a culture of stopping to fix problems, to get quality right the first time.
6. Standardized tasks and processes are the foundation for continuous improvement and employee empowerment.
7. Use visual control so no problems are hidden.
8. Use only reliable, thoroughly tested technology that serves your people and processes.

9. Grow leaders who thoroughly understand the work, live the philosophy, and teach it to others.
10. Develop exceptional people and teams who follow your company's philosophy.
11. Respect your extended network of partners and suppliers by challenging them and helping them improve.
12. Go and see for yourself to thoroughly understand the situation.
13. Make decisions slowly by consensus, thoroughly considering all options; then implement decisions rapidly.
14. Become a learning organization through relentless reflection and continuous improvement.

If we examine these principles carefully, we will see that most of these seem to fit into any industry. A great deal of organizational time and energy would be saved if some of these principles are followed.

Debashis Sarkar

In my own book *Lean for Service Organizations and Offices: A Holistic Approach for Achieving Operational Excellence* (ASQ Press, 2008), I delineated an approach for Lean implementation in the service sector. Targeted for service companies, the approach evolved from researching, experimenting and catalyzing Lean transformations in a service context. Called the DEB-LOREX™ Model, the approach has been summarized in Figure 1.1 and has been discussed in detail in Lesson 23.

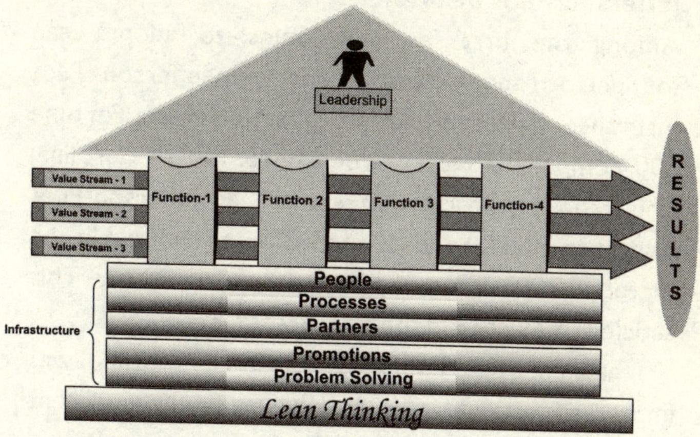

Fig 1.1: DEB-LOREX™ Model for Lean Transformation

The DEB-LOREX™ model is specifically targeted towards service companies.

Key Takeaways
■ The fundamental ideas of Lean are more critical than the industry specifics they are evolved or implemented in. ■ Looking at various contributions of thought leaders will help you look at Lean from various perspectives. ■ Lean is a new concept for service-oriented businesses and provides an opportunity to add to the existing body of knowledge.

FROM THE TRENCHES: Insurance

Jefferson Pilot Insurance

Among the first few companies to adopt Lean for performance improvement was Jefferson Pilot Insurance. Jefferson-Pilot Corporation was a Fortune 500 company based in Greensboro, North Carolina. The Lean transformation started at Jefferson-Pilot Insurance in 2000 and its success was reported in the October 2003 issue of *Harvard Business Review*. This article is a must-read for all practitioners.

I had an opportunity to visit their site and was impressed to see the results achieved by the intelligent customization of Lean principles from the manufacturing world. I could see the impressive gains achieved through Lean in areas such as fixed annuity operations; commissions; policy billing and collections; licensing and activation and call-centre operations.

The catalyst for the transformation was Cynthia Karen Swank who was then working as a Vice President. She was supported by an international consulting company. The company was acquired by Lincoln Financial group in March 2006. As reported in the *Harvard Business Review* article, some of the principles used were:

1. Building a model cell,
2. Placing linked processes near one another,
3. Standardizing procedures,
4. Eliminating loop-back,

(*Continued*)

5. Setting a common tempo,
6. Balancing loads,
7. Segregating complexity,
8. Posting performance results,
9. Setting performance goals.

(*Source*: Swank, Cynthia Karen, 'The Lean Service Machine', *Harvard Business Review*, Boston, Oct 2003.)

Lesson 3

THE CUSTOMER WILL NOT PAY FOR EVERYTHING IN A PROCESS

Processes are a set of activities that work in tandem to achieve a specific objective. These objectives could be called the **Process Mission** or **Process Objectives**. So quite simply put, the mission of a process is essentially the reason why it was devised and exists in the organization. The smallest unit of a process is a task.

It's important for managers and organizations to remember that all the tasks or steps that are done in a process may not add value. In a Lean project, the endeavour is to eradicate activities which the customer does not value. In the world of Lean management, everything that happens has to be scrutinized via the lens of the customer. The way to do this is to dissect the process and understand whether every activity that happens adds value to customer. The approach to be followed to identify non-value-adding steps in a process is to break it up into tasks and then question it from a customer's point of view.

Activities in the processes are broadly of three types. They are encapsulated in Table 1.1 (on the next page) with examples and how they should be treated under Lean.

Over a period of time, non-value added tasks in a process get branded as business-value-added. This is something that should be avoided at all costs. While doing a Lean evaluation, look closely at every business-value-added activity to determine if it is necessary for regulation and control or not.

Measure the times spent on value-added, non-value-added and business-value-added tasks. A metric used to track this is process efficiency, which is calculated as follows:

$$\textbf{Process Efficiency} = \frac{\textbf{Value-Added Time X 100}}{\textbf{(Value-Added Time + Non-Value-Added Time + Business-Value-Added Time)}}$$

Process Efficiency is also called the Value-Added Ratio. It makes sense to calculate the process efficiency of key processes in organizations every six to eight months. A services process which has not been looked at through the Lean lens can have process efficiency in single digits or even as low as one.

Table 1.1: Activities and their Values

	Value-Added	**Business-Value-Added**	**Non-Value-Added**
Definition of Activities	They are those tasks in a process for which the customer is willing to pay. These steps help to bring about a transformation in the product or service being provided by the organization and help to add a feature or trait which the customer values.	They are those tasks in a process for which the customers are not willing to pay but cannot be avoided. They necessarily need to be present in the process. They are also called: Necessary Non-Value-Add. They cannot be eliminated from the process. Typically these are activities done for quality control, meeting regulations and so on.	They are those activities in a process for which no customer is willing to pay nor should they. More importantly, these can be avoided.
Examples	• Data entry • Engaging with the customer	• Multiple levels of inspection • Re-checking of data entry	• Waiting • Loop-back of application forms
How should they be treated under Lean?	Optimize and standardize	Question and reduce	Eliminate

Key Takeaways

An activity/step in a process should meet all the following criteria to be treated as adding value:

- Should change the form, feature, feeling* and function which the customer cares for.
- Should be done right the first time.
- Should be something the customer is willing to pay for.

* Feeling is of great importance in service companies where there can be activities to improve the customer's experience.

Lesson 4

Cost-cutting is not Lean Thinking

Organizations often view Lean as purely a cost-cutting tool. This is a parochial view from individuals or organizations that do not entirely comprehend what Lean thinking is and what it can do to a business. Lean is not a cost-cutting tool but a method that drives cost-efficiency. This is not just an issue of semantics but an approach that should be followed in both the contexts of cost-cutting and cost efficiency. As we know, when we look at cutting costs the objective is to bring down costs by negotiations, management mandate or simply a management call.

For example, imagine a scenario where the travel costs in an organization have gone up almost 200 per cent over their budget. The management panics and decides to do something about it. The top management team meets and takes the following decisions in an effort to arrest the spiraling costs:

- Travel costs of all sales and service managers cut by 50 per cent (it was found that the sales and service managers travel the most).
- Travel per-diem allowances of all employees cut by 20 per cent.
- All employees to travel in low cost airlines.
- Anybody at middle management and below who travels more than twice in six months to require approval from a Vice President.
- During tours, employees to travel by public transport and avoid taking taxis/cabs.

What are the results? The costs come down by half but these measures affect business volumes drastically too. The volume of sales shows a downward trend and by the year end the business volumes also decrease by almost 40 per cent as sales managers substantially reduce travel (given the cost pressures). They virtually stop cold calls, which they had done quite frequently earlier, to acquire new customers. Also, the customer satisfaction levels drop radically. While the quality of products remains the same, the after-sales service deteriorates, as earlier, a visit by a service executive to a customer with problems not only led to quick resolutions but also created and cemented customer loyalty. But with the cost-cutting drive, the number of customer visits drops and this dents the perception of service in the customer's mind. On top of this, the unilateral policies of the company on travel alienate its employees. These are rather drastic measures for cost-cutting.

This example may seem rudimentary and you may think who in their right minds would practice Lean in this manner? But there are several such real-life examples in the business world. In a management philosophy, managers and leaders look for solutions for what they want and not what the philosophy recommends in its entirety.

If this organization was actually practicing Lean, it would have approached the problem differently and communicated the cost challenges to everyone. This would have been then followed by brainstorming about what processes contribute towards these escalating costs. Cost-cutting is not Lean management. Whenever costs go up, I would suggest that management should tell their teams to evaluate the process. If your organization is using 'activity-based costing', it can only add to this effort. While looking at the activities in the process the teams can use Table 1.2.

Table 1.2 Activities and their Treatment Under Lean

Activities	Approach under Lean
Value-Added	Improve and standardize
Business-Value-Added (Non-Value-Added but required)	Question and reduce
Non-Value-Added	Eliminate

The organization would then have asked the teams to apply Lean in each of these processes (Figure 1.2 on the facing page) to make them more effective.

This entire train of events would undoubtedly have been fairly time-consuming. However, it would have delivered fundamentally long-lasting benefits to the organization. Remember, Lean is about cost

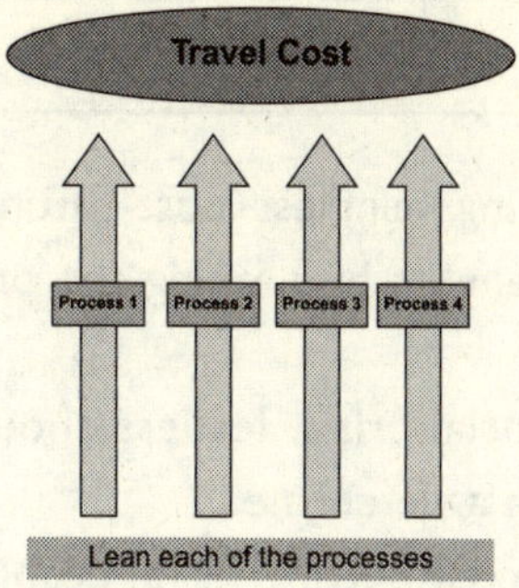

Fig 1.2: Lean and Travel Costs

leadership and entails the dissection of processes for performance enhancement. Unlike cost-cutting it is not a one-time exercise but something which has to be revisited at regular intervals. When you bring about cost efficiency in your businesses, it has far reaching results, beyond cost-cutting. Lean cost efficiency:

- Makes your customer happier (because costs may go down and the benefits could be passed on to them),
- Creates an engine of continual improvement wherein teams meet on a regular basis to question processes,
- Has the positive buy-in of the employees (unlike cost-cutting which is often unilateral or mandated from top),
- Brings about process thinking because whenever costs go up teams look at processes for improvement,
- Gives long-term and sustainable results,
- Increases the competitiveness of business,
- Makes the organization agile and nimble.

Key Takeaways

- Instead of doing mindless cost-cutting, achieve long-lasting cost benefits by Leaning the processes in your organization.
- During a financial crisis, leaders should look at Lean for creating an agile engine.
- By branding cost-cutting as a Lean intervention, a brilliant improvement engine such as Lean gets killed in an organization.

FROM THE TRENCHES: Lean impacts the cost-income ratios of financial institutions.

In a column in BusinessWeek.com dated March 6, 2009 it was reported that:

> Research done by Operational Council at the Corporate Executive Board found that institutions that implemented Lean are able to double the amount of cost-reduction opportunities they identify and operate more efficiently than their peers. Lean manufacturing concepts are relatively inexpensive to implement, are easy to understand, and often generate quick cost reductions.

The article further went on to report that:

> Financial institutions applying Lean techniques to their operations have reported 20-40 per

(*Continued*)

cent cost reductions in as little time as 12 to 18 months. In addition, many Lean adopters are able to realize employee productivity gains of more than 30 per cent. In the current environment, Lean represents a powerful tool for reducing expenses while also strengthening customer relationships.

(*Source*: www.businessweek.com dated March 6, 2009, 2:08PM EST)

Lesson 5

ADOPT A QUIVER APPROACH

While managers love to talk about Lean, its implementation often suffers from the misunderstanding of two critical issues.

1) Overemphasis on the tools and methodology of Lean

It would be quite short-sighted to look at Lean from a tools and techniques perspective. That is hardly the core of Lean. Managers must position Lean as an overarching philosophy to drive business improvements in the organization. Let the overall improvement philosophy subsume the specific methodologies.

The biggest mistake is made when the improvement methodology becomes larger than the outcomes that it is supposed to produce. Remember, Lean is an approach to achieve business results. While you make your company efficient by adopting Lean tools and practices, the larger objective should be to achieve the goals that the organization sets for itself.

As a change agent responsible for driving excellence in operations, your agenda should be to achieve business outcomes. While you toil to achieve competence on the tools and techniques, never lose sight of the larger objectives. I have seen Lean Navigators spending a lot of time using tools for no other reason but because they are available. Discourage teams who force-fit tools in the projects impacting timelines and final results. It is good to achieve mastery in specific tools but it can never be done at the cost of final results. Business leaders and Lean Mavens have to keep a close eye to make sure this does not happen.

2) Assuming a single approach has all the answers

While you implement Lean in your company, it would be parochial to think that a single methodology will be able to solve all your problems. Remember, a one-size-fits-all strategy does not work. Based on the types of problems, specific methodologies have to be used. This is required to ensure that an optimal approach is followed to get the best results.

What organizations need to do is to follow an integrated approach to improvement. Lean can be the overarching improvement cry but build a **quiver approach**.

So, what's a quiver approach?

The quiver approach is about creating competencies in multiple methodologies within the organization.

Let the organization build competencies in key methodologies and tools such as Lean, Six Sigma, Theory of Constraints, TRIZ (Theory of Inventive Problem Solving), Poka-Yoke, Process Management, 5S etc. These are like the arrows which are kept in the quiver before they are taken out to target an enemy. The analogy is that the arrows (methodologies) are of different colours which are to be used for enemies (problems) of varying hues/types.

Institutionalizing the quiver approach is not easy. Organizations are like crowds and herds – literally. They love single mantras and single buzzwords. Asking them to be incisive and meditative about problem-solving is extremely difficult. It also takes time, as building competencies in multiple improvement approaches requires patience and management commitment. It would require the investment of time and money which at times management may find difficult to condone.

However, business leaders serious about building a robust foundation for driving operational excellence understand its necessity. Some leaders argue that they should build competence in the most relevant methodology. For everything else, consultants can be hired. This is a deeply flawed approach because improvements can never be outsourced. Consultants can and should be used as guides to build competencies within the firm but they never should be used to carry out improvements on behalf of the firm. This is counterproductive to never letting that problem happen again.

Table 1.3 (on the facing page) summarizes the various types of problems and improvement

Table 1.3: Problem Type and Improvement Methodology

S No	Problem Type	Description	Methodology
1	Ineffective Output	Process not meeting the requirements of the customers.	Six Sigma
2	Unsystematic Process	Tasks are getting done but there is a need for structured approach to execute tasks.	Business Process Management System, Standard Work
3	Inefficient Process	Process laden with inefficiency and there is an opportunity to optimize the usage of resources.	Lean
4	Tribal Process	Work is getting done but there is no defined process. Knowledge is confined to the process-owner or a few people.	Business Process Management System, Standard Work
5	Complexity Inundation	Organization or process laden with complexity.	Lean, Complexity Reduction
6	Non-Existent Process	Need for a new process for a new product or service. This is related to design of new process.	DMADV, Lean Product Development
7	Workplace Irritants	Small local improvements are needed.	7 QC Tools, Why-Why Analysis
8	Inept Product or Service	Product or service not able to meet the requirements of the customer.	Lean Product Development, DMADV

methodologies that can be adopted by companies. The problem type refers to a situation where there is a deficiency or gap from the desired state. The list may not be all-encompassing for manufacturing but is quite comprehensive for service-oriented businesses.

To summarize, make your company's methodology eclectic. Let Lean be used as a larger improvement philosophy. Adopt the quiver approach. Build an array of competencies which help the organization to solve a wide variety of problems in variety of contexts.

Key Takeaways
■ Follow an integrated approach to operational excellence. Leverage multiple methodologies but keep your eyes firmly on the larger purpose of the organization. ■ Create competencies in multiple improvement methodologies in your company. ■ Before adopting an improvement method, understand the context and ascertain what exactly is needed. ■ Sometimes it may make sense to name a Lean journey a performance improvement or something else which the company is comfortable with. This is to avoid getting into a methodology trap.

FROM THE TRENCHES: Varied organizations, varied results

Shinhan Bank

Shinhan Bank applied Lean techniques to integrate operations following its 2006 merger with Chohung Bank and became one of Korea's leading commercial lenders.

BMO Financial Group

The BMO Financial Group's Bank of Montreal credits its Lean Six Sigma work with freeing up $55 million in cost savings which it can reinvest in growth.

(*Source*: Guarraia, Peter and Andrew Schwedel, *For Banks in Need: Getting More from Lean Six Sigma*, published by Bain and Company, 2008)

Lesson 6

Know the Fundamental Differences between Service and Manufacturing Processes

Lean can be applied to services but it is not as easy as it seems to be. Given the complex structure of service processes they provide particular challenges which a Lean change agent should be aware of. Many of these challenges arise because service processes function in a different way:

Service processes may not be visible:

Manufacturing processes are visible and we see resources (input) getting converted to product (output). This is however, not the case with service processes. Inputs and resources that are used in service processes may not be always tangible. Hence, it is critical to define and identify the basic contours of the process before it is taken up for Lean treatment. This is especially true for service processes which are not very old and no effort has been taken to document them for future reference. The problems further escalate when technology is used as an enabler in service processes. For a rookie to understand such a process is not easy. This is where tools such as SIPOC-R[1] are of great help.

Service processes are manpower intensive:

One of the key resources used in service processes is people. Their contribution is the key towards meeting the objectives of the process. This is not easy as it requires committed and motivated people to work efficiently and meet larger objectives. Tools and techniques can improve processes; however, they can be sustained only by reorienting the behaviour of teams so that they proactively look for wastes and work towards eliminating them. This is where a Lean intervention has to move from mere process improvements to being a part of the organizational culture.

Service processes may not have metrics:

Tracking the performance of service processes is still a relatively new idea in many industries. Most often performance evaluation of processes is reactive, based on quality of outcomes or customer feedback/ complaints. Such processes lack effective metrics to continuously track the performance and health of processes. In such a situation we first need to baseline the process, to understand its state, before taking it up for improvement.

[1] SIPOC-R stands for Supplier, Input, Process, Output, Customer and Requirement.

Identifying waste may not be easy:

Given the invisible nature of service processes, identifying wastes in them is not easy. Often symptoms of wastes and inefficiencies may not be as overt as in manufacturing companies. There could be lots of emails, data, information, papers, documents, and redundant procedures which are visible only to highly trained eyes. One has to learn to spot these not-so-obvious wastes. This is where value-stream mapping[2] is of great help as discussed in greater detail in later lessons.

Output of customer-facing processes cannot be corrected:

In a manufacturing context, poor product quality can often be rectified before it reaches the customer. In services, however, especially for customer-facing processes, the output gets delivered to the customer instantly with hardly any opportunity for corrections. So, service processes have to be impeccable and virtually error-free. If errors occur, there has to be a solid service recovery process so that the dissatisfaction of the customer can be converted into a business opportunity. Also, for the customer-facing processes, the process itself is the product as the customer does not just experience the product but also experiences the process that is used to deliver the product. It is the experience which matters and is an integral part of the service product. Every service product requirement is difficult and should always

[2] Value-stream mapping is an approach to identify wastes in process.

include the emotional component. This becomes critical as Lean improvements have to be targeted towards meeting the objectives of the customer. Service is after all about people.

Layout design objectives are quite different:

Lean is all about creating flow and this is where we endeavour to create a suitable layout. The objectives of creating process layout in both manufacturing and service companies are quite different. The primary objective of layouts in manufacturing is the reduction in transport time. In a services set-up the primary objectives would be employee productivity enhancement, reduction of communication costs (such as in a back office processing) and greater customer convenience (such as in a bank).

Key Takeaways
■ Processes in service businesses can be mired in challenges which may not be there in manufacturing. ■ Leaning a service process can be challenging as many times the processes may not be visible. ■ Service processes are at times manpower intensive so their engagement in the Lean journey is very critical. ■ Installing metrics is sometimes the first step in a Lean journey.

Lesson 7

Not Just Metrics But the Right Metrics

In the manufacturing sector it is quite common to measure the performance of processes on a continual basis. The processes are visible and measuring them comes quite naturally. Also, the improvement journey of the manufacturing processes has been under continual scrutiny for more than sixty years.

The story is quite different in the service sector. The journey of improvements in service sector is not very old and relevant processes may not always have the required metrics. Processes in the service sector are often not visible which makes it difficult to even appreciate that an activity is a process. This is especially true for functions which are traditionally not thought to be driven by processes such as sales, human resources, marketing and finance.

However, things are changing and service sector companies have begun installing metrics. But when scrutinized closely, one often finds that the metrics are not relevant. The problem is that the focus is often on installing metrics and not on the benefit they will deliver. So, metrics are installed, they get measured, man-hours are spent on analyzing them but they do not deliver much value. Thus despite the intentions being good, organizations inadvertently create waste which could have been avoided if they had looked at installing the right metrics. This is what I call the waste of measurement system.

So, what are the pointers that companies should remember before installing metrics? I call them the A to H principles of installing relevant and waste-free metrics in a company on a journey towards Lean transformation. Table 1.4 summarizes Debashis's or Deb's A to H principles of installing the right metrics in an organization.

Table 1.4: Deb's A to H Principles of Metrics

	Attribute	What does it mean?
A	Action Oriented	The metrics should be presented in such a manner that process associates can comprehend them easily and take action. This can be achieved by following the traffic light colours of red, yellow and green, to represent performance.
B	Big Picture Connect	The metrics should be aligned with strategic business objectives. This should include meeting the expectations of shareholders, partners, customers, regulators, employees and the society.
C	Customer Led	The metrics should meet customer requirements and should have linkages with operational levers.

Table 1.4: Deb's A to H Principles of Metrics (*Continued*)

	Attribute	What does it mean?
D	Digitized	Avoid manual data collection processes. Even if it takes time, gradually the organization should move towards automated data collection which later gets converted to digitized dashboards.
E	Employee Involvement	Whatever metrics are used, it is imperative that they should have the involvement of the employees. It's okay to use an outside resource/consultant/member of the Lean office as a facilitator, but never push for the metrics without the buy-in of the employees.
F	Familiar	The metrics should be standardized across business units of an organization. There should be a common currency which helps everyone understand the process performance irrespective of functions and levels.
G	Guiding	The metrics should include leading and causal indicators that help in predicting the outcomes of the process and allow action to be taken before something goes wrong.
H	Holistic	They should be end-to-end metrics cutting across silos which give a holistic approach to measure the way the process performs.

I would recommend that business leaders/value stream owners ascertain the overall effectiveness of their measurement system. This can be done by following the template shown in Table 1.5 on the facing page. The blank spaces can be populated by using the scoring pattern given at the end of the template.

Table 1.5 Template for Metrics Effectiveness

	Attribute	**Value Stream/ Process 1**	**Value Stream/ Process 2**	**Value Stream/ Process 3**	**Value Stream/ Process 4**	**Value Stream/ Process 5**
A	Action Oriented					
B	Big Picture Connect					
C	Customer Led					
D	Digitized					
E	Employee Involvement					
F	Familiar					
G	Guiding					
H	Holistic					

Scoring Pattern

What is it	**Score**
Does not Exist	1
Partially Exists	3
Fully Exists	7

Interpretation:

The following table (Table 1.6) could be used to interpret the scores. Remember, this is only directional and essentially tells you how far you are from an effective measurement system.

Table 1.6 Interpretation of Scores for Effective Metrics Management

Score	Interpretation
More than 49	The measurement system is effective for creating a Lean organization.
36-48	The measurement system is partially effective.
22-35	The measurement system is just being built and a lot is left to do.
Less than 21	The measurement system is not effective.

Having installed metrics it is quite futile for organizations to stay with them forever. Typically what happens is that once metrics get installed, no one questions them. All that happens is that newer metrics just get added to the existing ones and the list keeps on increasing. This especially happens after an improvement project is completed. As a result the processes get inundated. Prioritizing the important ones becomes difficult. Added to this is the fear that if metrics are removed the performance of the process would be affected.

A good Lean organization continually questions the relevance of metrics to the business. Remember, metrics are just an enabler to business improvement; they cannot become the business of an organization.

Install a system wherein the metrics get reviewed on a regular basis so that redundant metrics are done away with, and newer ones are installed wherever required. I would recommend that all service organizations should refresh their metrics once a year.

Key Takeaways

- An ineffective measurement system can steer you in the wrong direction. Beware!
- It is important to assess the metrics installed in your processes with the A to H principles.
- Refresh the metrics on a regular basis – at least once a year. This is because what is relevant today may not be of use tomorrow.
- Despite highly performing metrics, sometimes problems in processes continue. This could be because the right metrics may not be installed.

Lesson 8

Begin Your Journey with a Holistic Roadmap

Having decided to leverage Lean as way of doing business, where do you begin? This is a question often faced by business leaders. An incorrect approach or advice can mar the deployment of this practice. Table 1.7 (on the facing page) summarizes the broad roadmap for implementing Lean in a company. This could take anywhere from five to ten years. For details I would recommend you to refer to my book: *Lean for Service Organizations and Offices: A Holistic Approach for Achieving Operational Excellence* (ASQ Press, Milwaukee, 2008).

Table 1.7: Broad Roadmap for Implementation

S No	What	Details
1	Lean Leadership Session	Session to share the potential and possibility of Lean in delivering business benefits.
2	Vision	This refers to the vision the organisation has for itself and how Lean can enable this acheivement.
3	Deployment Roadmap	Script a detailed roadmap for deployment of the Lean principles.
4	Lean Office	Create a central Lean office to catalyze improvements.
5	Install Anchors	Install anchors to embed Lean thinking within the company.
6	Lean Navigators	Create Lean Navigators who will act as change agents for Lean within business units and value streams.
7	Awareness Creation	Create awareness among all employees on the Lean journey and how to learn to see waste.
8	Value Streams	Identify the value streams within business units
9	Core Process Identification	Identify the core processes within each of the value streams.
10	Process Owners	Appoint process owners who manage end-to-end processes and cross-functional issues.
11	Process Metrics	Install relevant metrics to ascertain the ongoing health of process performance.
12	Large Improvement Projects (LIP)	Large improvement projects are taken up for value stream mapping followed by a large number of Lean breakthroughs.

Table 1.7: Broad Roadmap for Implementation (*Continued*)

S No	What	Details
13	Process Improvement within Silos	Lean is used for improving processes but this is confined to the respective silos/functions.
14	Small Improvement Projects (SIP)	Small Improvement Projects are launched to facilitate improvements at the grassroot levels.
15	End-to-end Process Improvements	Core processes which cut across functional silos and departments are taken up for improvement.
16	Lean for Business Ends	Lean practice starts in value streams and business units to meet strategic business objectives and achieve the aspirational state of the company.
17	Lean for Product and Process Development	Use Lean for developing new products and services.
18	Redefine Aspirational State	Having made gains, it may be apt to redefine the new level of the aspiration state.

The approach table is not necessarily sequential. It should also be noted that only the key steps are mentioned. At a conceptual level, the outcomes of Lean happen in broad four phases which are shown in Figure 1.3. Remember, the metrics for each of the phases would be different so performance is measured based on the context and maturity of implementation. If the company has a large number of business units, the type of Lean actions will be based on the maturity of its Lean implementation.

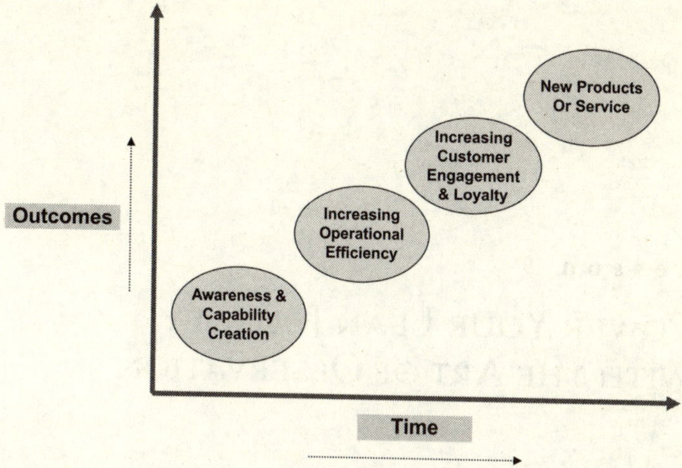

Fig 1.3: Outcomes of Lean Over Time

Key Takeaways
■ Implementation of Lean requires many initiatives which have to be joined together to deliver business impact. ■ Lean journeys often go astray because of lack of a complete roadmap. ■ While scripting the roadmap for Lean, do keep in mind current and future challenges/opportunities. ■ Use Lean not just for improving processes and business-systems; leverage it also for new product/process design. ■ Actions from a Lean intervention will vary based on the maturity and type of business units.

Lesson 9

Power Your Lean Journey with the Art of Observation

Mastering the art of observation is a key aspect in Lean implementation. In this lesson we will discuss the power of observations which are an integral part of Ground Zero Walks.[3]

As a part of Lean implementation, business leaders, value-stream owners, Lean mavens, and all employees should master the art of observation. This is not easy and the organizational leadership has to really invest time to master it.

What is an observation?

Observation refers to what you see in a workplace or a certain context as you walk through it or are a

[3] The term Ground Zero Walk first appeared in my book *Quality in Business* (Sage, 2003).

part of it. Observation is an art and has to be mastered under an able expert. This cannot happen through a leadership mandate; teams have to be taught how to do it.

The following are a few objectives which are accomplished through observation:

- See at source what is happening,
- Unfurl potential problems,
- Get a feel of what's the real workplace – see beyond the obvious,
- Ascertain the health of Lean deployment,
- Look beyond what teams present to leaders,
- Connect with the teams who are at the *Gemba* (or the workplace) where the action is happening,
- Understand the components which make up the context,
- Get beyond data, into facts,
- Piece together visual images to get a pulse of the organization,
- Understand the customer,
- Understand what is working and what is not in the organization.

Shoji Shiba's book, *Breakthrough Management,* talks about the three key guidelines for improving observations:

- Go to the source,
- Focus on specific objects and elements,
- Identify interrelationships among the object and the elements.

The works of Shoji Shiba and Gerald F. Smith provide a great insight into how the power of observation can be used for workplace improvement. Table 1.8 summarizes the approach which I have been following for carrying out an observation. Observation means looking at visual, audio, tactile and olfactory senses.

Table 1.8: Deb's 10 Rules for Workplace Observation

S No	Rule	What is it	Examples
1	Closely peruse the source	Look at the workplace closely and find out what is happening. Look at how things are done, the interactions among the teams, the workplace condition and the mood of the workplace and teams.	During a visit to an office look at the condition of the workplace. Have files, documents been kept in order?
2	Look at the periphery	Look at places beyond the current workplace. Find out what is happening in the environment around the workplace.	While visiting a bank check the cleanliness of the toilet, the tidiness of the external area around the branch and the condition of car parking.
3	Look for issues without ownership	Look for processes or any other item which does not have ownership.	Despite tall claims by management about process ownership, in one example I was able to find a few processes with no one looking after them.
4	Look for abnormalities	Are there issues which are abnormal and should not be there? Often a problem may not appear on the surface and all will seem to be quite right.	• In one example I found a small leak in the corner of the wall. On investigation, later, it was found that there were structural issues in the building which needed to be taken care of immediately.

Table 1.8: Deb's 10 Rules for Workplace Observation (*continued*)

S No	Rule	What is it	Examples
			• In the kitchen of a leading hotel I smelled something awful. It emerged that the kitchen had a problem with the exhaust.
5	Look at your customers	Watch how your customers experience your product or service. Sometimes it means having to meet the toughest customers.	Observe how the customers are treated by the sales executives. See how conveniently the customers get their desired product or service. Specifically, look at their facial expressions.
6	Look for what's missing	Unfurl what is missing in the workplace. This requires looking beyond the obvious.	While facilitating a Lean project meeting, I found the teams to be quiet. The reason was that the business unit had a command and control culture wherein nobody spoke in front of their superiors.
7	Look for symptoms	Look for symptoms or signals which indicate potential problems.	While looking at a large hospital, I found large number of unplanned casual-leaves being taken. I found that the team was highly de-motivated and lacked a sense of ownership for their workplace.
8	Look at people's behaviour	See how people are behaving and talking to each other. It is a manifestation of past and current experiences.	A process owner of a leading organization told me how proud he was that no problems had been reported to him for the last six months as the

Table 1.8: Deb's 10 Rules for Workplace Observation (*continued*)

S No	Rule	What is it	Examples
			process had become highly efficient. Later it was discovered that the culture of the company was such that reporting problems was taboo. Individuals got rebuked when they reported workplace problems – this is very anti-Lean.
9	Look for legacies and remnants of the past	See if there are remnants from the past which tell something about the company or the workplace. Something which happened in the past can have linkages with the present.	While walking through the front-office of an international hotel chain, I saw a large queue to check-in. On probing it came out that the IT system used for checking-in guests was slow. Later I discovered that this property had recently been acquired and the IT system had not been upgraded.
10	Do comparisons	Compare existing practices, standards and data from within the company against other companies which you may have seen. This could throw up opportunities for action.	In a bank back-office which sent monthly account statements to customers, it was found that the company was using an expensive international courier. On comparison with another low cost local courier, it was discovered that both took the same time to deliver the documents to the customer and the defect levels were also the same. This comparison led to the bank changing to the local courier resulting in cost savings. A little comparison can lead to such a great improvement.

Many of the points mentioned in Table 1.8 could overlap. Do not worry about the categories they fall into, just go ahead and observe. Often you have to use a mix of several rules to come to a conclusion.

When you begin with observations it makes immense sense to get coached under an expert who is adept in observation skills. Just remember, every aspect of the organization provides an opportunity for observation. If required, ask a few questions in a non-threatening manner. Sometimes, observation is about unlearning a lot of things. Never allow what you know to overshadow your observations. Look at everything with a child's mind and a lot of curiosity. And yes, listen, listen and listen.

Remember, mastering the art of observation requires practice and takes many years. If you are serious about implementing Lean, inculcate this habit amongst all your employees. Of course, observation has to be followed by evaluation, analysis and inference.

Key Takeaways
■ The act of observation can reveal a lot about the company. ■ Observation means looking at visual, audio, tactile and olfactory senses. ■ In service businesses, you have to sometimes use your observation power even in the virtual world.

- Not using the power of observation of your employees means squandering the latent value which your employees can deliver to the organization. Train all your employees on Deb's Ten Rules for Workplace Observation.

Lesson 10

Process Should Positively Impact the Key Stakeholders

We have discussed processes in Lesson 3. We all know that processes are an integral part of product or service delivery. Processes comprise input, output, procedures, tasks and policies. Creating standardized processes is a must for many parts of service businesses.[4] Standard processes have to be installed across service delivery centres to ensure consistent delivery of product or service to the customers.

However, when we talk about a process, we do not only keep **customers** in mind. Our sole objective is to create a good process so that it meets the requirements of the customer it serves. There is also a lot of effort to ensure that the process meets the needs of the **business**. Organizations spend a lot of

[4] Except for customer-facing processes, as discussed in Lesson 53.

energy to achieve this objective, and teams succeeding in these projects get celebrated with much hype.

However, we often seem to forget a key stakeholder whom the processes serve. Beyond the customer and business, the processes need to serve the **people who run them**. In our urgency to meet the other requirements, we seem to forget what a process should do or be for the individuals who work on it. Remember, it is the people who give life to the process so meeting their requirements is the key. While designing processes, it is imperative that they should positively impact all the three key stakeholders: customer, business and people.

A good process should have the following impact on the people who run it:

- Makes process execution easy,
- Is easy to follow,
- Has smooth flow and there is minimal or no back-and-forth action/loop-back,
- Easy to adopt and adapt for ongoing execution,
- Helps to train the uninitiated,
- Helps to get more from less resources,
- Breaks down silos and builds cross-functional coordination,
- Improves team efficiency and effectiveness (Efficiency helps to deliver more from less; Effectiveness helps to meet the objectives of the team).

A process improvement which positively impacts only one or two of the three stakeholders can be quite sub-optimal and the fullest outcome from the process may not be achieved. This is also a reason why the designing and improvement of a process should always happen with the involvement of the teams who run it.

Table 1.9 is a short questionnaire which leaders can answer on their processes to see if they have been designed or improved to positively impact all three stakeholders or not. Answering 'yes' to all the questions will mean that the process is suitably designed or optimized.

Table 1.9: Deb's Questionnaire on Effectiveness of Process Optimization

	Questions	Yes/No
Customer: The recipient of the product or service produced by the process		
1	Is the process helping to meet the requirements of the customer (requirements comprise: cost, speed, quality, safety, convenience etc)?	
2	Is the process making it easy for the customer to interact with the organization?	
Business: The larger entity which houses the process and works towards meeting certain objectives		
1	Is the process making a positive impact of the business objectives/workplace performance?	
2	Is the process the most efficient and cost-effective way of accomplishing the results?	
People: The individuals who are involved in running the process		
1	Is the process supporting the performance of the people who run it?	
2	Is the process making it easy for the team to run it?	
3	Was it designed and implemented with their involvement?	

Key Takeaways

- While carrying out process improvements it could be myopic to focus only on customers. A process improvement should positively impact the customer, business and people.
- Use Deb's questionnaire to ascertain the effectiveness of your process optimization.
- If your process improvement does not make it easy for the people who run it, it indicates an incomplete endeavour.

Lesson 11

Service Guarantees can be a Good Aspiration

Offering a service guarantee can be a good goal to engage a company on a Lean transformation journey. While this may not be the only mission of a company, it creates sufficient pressure on the company to make its processes not only effective but also efficient enough to meet the objectives. I have seen service guarantees be quite inspirational for driving operational excellence through Lean, as they require a focus on customer, product and process design. This is not easy and requires relevant processes cutting across silos to function at a certain level of performance.

So what is a service guarantee?

It is an unconditional promise made to the customer which assures that if the pre-defined service delivery standards are not met, the company will compensate the customer. When you guarantee a product or service to a customer, it means that you are promising to fulfill your claims. For example, a bank might promise to its customers that in its branches, the teller will deliver cash in three minutes. It will then compensate the customers with $5 for every occasion when the customer does not get the money in time.

Why have a guarantee?

A customer guarantee can not only differentiate a company but actually create a solid working engine of Lean management. The target of meeting a customer guarantee is so powerful that it can integrate the whole organization towards the larger objective of customer satisfaction. It drives consumer focused improvements that in turn positively influence the behaviour of existing, potential and dissatisfied customers. The practices of Lean just become an enabler here. However, achieving such a target would require working on all aspects of customer delivery such as people, policies, processes, technology, infrastruture, experience, measurements and so on. It would require organizational leadership to take action on tacit issues of complexity management, process handoffs, process workaround, silo issues, etc. I call them tacit issues because companies often do not focus on them but they are critical to superior customer service.

Table 1.10 summarizes a few to-dos that need to be adopted while offering a service guarantee.

Table 1.10: To-Dos For Customer Guarantees

To Do	Details
Select a Product/Product Family	Based on the market scan, customer segment and customer needs, select a product or a product family. During the early days go slow and do not take too many products. Channelize all resources to ensure that the promise is delivered.
A Shared Vision	Begin with the CEO/Value-Stream Owner/Business Head creating a shared vision and clearly stating that customer guarantee will be a service differentiator and a key focus area for the next few years. The top management should communicate to all the employees the need and reason for a guarantee.
Voice of the Customer	Listen to what the customer actually requires. This is needed to design the right product or service, and to get feedback when the product is launched. Create an ongoing feedback system using multiple methods among different customer groups. Very often organizations adopt a single methodology and believe that they have a comprehensive approach to get the customer's feedback. Any single approach is inadequate as each has its own limitations. Based on the requirement, leverage the power of approaches such as transactional surveys, global surveys, mystery shopping, declining and lost customer surveys, focus group interviews, customer advisory panels, customer complaints/comments, employee surveys and so on.
Focus on Value-Stream	Focus on the value stream which will be used to deliver the product or service for which the customer guarantee will be provided. Find out the wastes within each of the core processes within this value stream. This will highlight the areas for improvement and the future state that needs to be achieved for offering the guarantee.
All Processes need not be Perfect	Do not wait for all processes to be perfect. Focus on improving the vital few value-creating processes which have a direct impact on the customer and the proposed service guarantee. Improve these processes with the customer's expectations in mind and work towards reducing the potential fail-points.

Table 1.10: To-Dos for Customer Guarantees (*Continued*)

To Do	Details
Customer Service Specialists	Develop competent customer service executives who are able to provide flawless service to customers. These individuals are not just trained on product or service characteristics but also on the way customers, moods and emotions are managed. Adequate doses of soft skills should be imparted to them. Empower them to take instant decisions on customer complaints/queries.
Make Guarantees Unconditional	A well-designed service guarantee should be unconditional. There should not be any exceptions or conditional qualifiers associated with it. There should not be any asterisks or ifs or buts. An example of a good guarantee states: *When you do business with Sierra Trading Post, you're getting the best guarantee out there. If you are not happy with your purchase for any reason, please return it to us for a full refund or exchange. This guarantee never expires! If you feel we have made a mistake in filling your order, we will gladly refund your shipping charges as well.*
Clarity of guarantees	Ensure that your promise to the customer is clear and explicit. It should not be open to any interpretation. The promise has to be pointed, sharp and the customer should clearly know the compensation associated with the service failure.
Attractiveness of Guarantee	Make sure that the compensation associated with the guarantee should be attractive enough for the customer to invoke it if dissatisfied. Do not make it so measly that the customer deems it to be not worth the effort.
Customer feedback process	Ensure that the process of getting the compensation is hassle free. The process should really be Lean – it should not only be fast but also give the customer a good feeling.
Focus on specific facets of the service at a time	In the early days, do not target all aspects of service around which the guarantee needs to be threaded. You can just focus on one aspect of a service, such as the lead time to deliver cash for the bank teller. However, as processes mature, all aspects of service can be covered such as the full satisfaction guarantee that is provided by a hotel.

Key Takeaways

- Offering a service guarantee will require your processes to be virtually pain-free.
- The goal of meeting a customer guarantee can propel the whole organization towards a larger purpose using the principles and practices of Lean thinking.
- Implementing a service guarantee will force a company to look at both the effectiveness and the efficiency of a process.
- The journey to achieving the service guarantee will not only facilitate cross-functional working, but also provide something which delights everyone – the customer, the business and the employees.

Lesson 12

Do Not Always Brand the Method of Change

Over the years, I have seen quite a few leaders who are averse to methodologies of change. When told that the organization needs a Lean intervention, they take it as another tool that the improvement practitioners peddle for getting their mindshare. They could retort by questioning the effectiveness of earlier initiatives such as Six Sigma, Elementary Problem Solving (7 QC Tools), Process Management etc.

This is where you need to get a sense of the organizational thinking. If you believe that leaders are averse to specific methods of improvements, just rename the deployment of Lean management techniques as something which suits the organization. Companies use different names for their drives for 'operational excellence', 'process excellence', 'performance improvement', 'business improvement' etc. At a leading bank, the Lean roll-out within the branch banking channel was called 'Symphony'. A telecom service provider calls its Lean roll-out 'Fast-Forward'. A manufacturing corporation calls its 'Velocity'.

However, what needs to be kept in mind is that the philosophies of Lean thinking should be embedded underneath. The key ones, which all service companies need to keep in mind while rolling out Lean, are:

- Keep in mind the impact your decisions will have on the company in the next 10, 15, 25, 50 and 100 years.
- Make your company outward-focused rather being inward-focused—keep the customers in mind in everything you do.
- Have respect for people.
- Always keep an eye on the impact being made on the community.
- Make sure that the laws (regulations etc) of the land are adhered to at all costs.
- Positively impact all stakeholders such as customers, shareholders, partners etc.
- Faced with a problem? Evaluate the process.
- Create leaders at all levels who live the company's philosophy.
- Embed the workplaces with processes and procedures.
- Make things simple.
- Create a culture of continuous improvement, value-stream thinking and constant reflection.
- All decisions and changes should be done with the team's involvement.

- Make the company unapproachable to all types of fraudsters, money-launderers etc.
- Ruthlessly protect the knowledge of the company.
- Use Lean transformation as an opportunity to identify talent for the company.

Remember, what is important is practicing the philosophy of Lean management and not losing sight of the primary objective by fighting over a name. Instead of calling your improvement teams Lean Mavens, Six Sigma Belts etc, you could call them Change Agents. As a Lean change agent you need to understand the minds of the CEO and other top leaders. Many times they may not be overt about their dislike; however this has to be ascertained by all means. The best thing to do is to let the name emerge from the company. You could run a contest and let an employee name it!

Key Takeaways
■ Let the name emerge from the organization. ■ Listen to the CEOs and other top leaders before you make a decision on the name. ■ Don't waste time squabbling over what the Lean rollout should be named – do what suits your company.

Section 2

People

PEOPLE

People are at the heart of Lean deployment. Getting the mindshare and engagement of teams is probably the biggest challenge faced during a Lean journey. Lean is not just about getting a set of tools and using them within the firm. It is about engaging employees to adopt and adapt the practices that weave a Lean fabric. Building a Lean culture comprises building a culture of process thinking, continual improvement and problem solving. Engaging people in this entails making sure employees across hierarchies get involved in the transformation. Individuals at each level have different roles to play. For example, the top management's major focus should be on the strategic aspects of Lean transformation while the middle management should spend a lot of time on tactical components.

It's the people who make the culture; and Lean management is about bringing about a common culture which is centred around respect for people, continual improvement and process thinking. This is not easy and takes years to impregnate the organizational fabric. Today if Toyota is known for its culture, it is because of the efforts it has put in over many years. As Edgar Shein (1984) and later Jeffrey Liker (2008) have taught us, culture has three levels comprising **Artifacts, Norms and Values** and **Underlying Assumptions. Artifacts** are those that are seen on the surface by people. **Norms** are the accepted rules of behaviour while **Values** are the principles we live by. **Underlying Assumptions** are unconscious or subconscious taken-for-granted beliefs about the company. Focusing on all the three levels is critical for organizational success.

What I hear, I forget.
What I see, I remember.
What I do, I understand.

—Confucius

CHAPTER 13

Lean Can not Solely be the Top Management's Agenda

It is not difficult to understand that Lean has to be driven by top management. (When I talk about top management, I am not referring only to the CEO but to the people who report directly to him or her also). Without the mindshare of the top management, it may be futile to start a Lean transformation. When we talk about leadership engagement, it has to be much more than just doing lip service. I have seen many CEOs saying all the right things in their speeches but if you talk about investing time to find out what's going on, their calendar is suddenly filled with meetings.

A CEO does remain busy with important things. However, if s/he believes that Lean implementation is important, s/he will surely find time. After all a CEO will only be busy with things that are deemed important. Merely feeling good about commencing on a Lean journey is not sufficient. What top leaders should do is to ensure that Lean is leveraged not only for bottom-line gains but also for achieving other strategic business objectives.

A CEO interested in Lean has to demonstrate a visible commitment to Lean and this can be done in many ways:

- Creating a shared vision on what the transformation of Lean would lead to,
- Spending time reviewing progress on a regular basis,
- Making a public commitment about the percentage profit improvement that will be brought about by Lean,
- Making all direct-reportees to the CEO responsible for Lean transformation in the company,
- Tying the outcomes of Lean transformation to the performance management scorecard of all top leaders,
- Undergoing leadership programmes on Lean management,
- Working to overcome the non-alignment at the top,
- Not jettisoning personal commitment when the chips are down.

However, it should be noted that getting leadership commitment is necessary but not sufficient. In today's world when the life of the CEO has reduced, just having the CEO's and top management's commitment may be quite short-sighted.

In such a context, what we need is a plan which ensures that there is adequate engagement at the top, the middle management and at the grassroots.

While top management has largely a strategic role in a Lean journey, the middle management makes it happen. It is quite imperative to have an engagement strategy to convert these individuals to agents of change. Lesson 22 discusses thoughts on middle-management engagement.

The ranks below middle management, the front-liners and grassroots employees all have to be simultaneously taken on board. This should happen at the early stage of implementation. The worst thing is to leave them to read the top management's mind on the proposed transformation. If they are not engaged, the teams can speculate on adverse possibilities such as layoffs, a hidden agenda from top management and so on. The onus is on the top management to ensure that the rank-and-file are engaged. They cannot be treated mechanically if we expect them to add to and contribute in the Lean transformation journey. The real agenda needs to be communicated and the teams trained on the foundations of Lean thinking. This has to be backed by supporting structures which allow teams to operate within the new behaviour.

Remember, Lean has to be for the people, by the people and of the people.

Key Takeaways

- It is the duty of the CEO to get closely involved in the Lean journey with employees.
- A successful Lean transformation is not possible without the equal participation of top management, middle management and the rank-and-file of the organization.
- Creating a powerful coalition is one of the first steps in a Lean transformation.
- Proactively look for individuals who do not seem to be engaged in the transformation.

FROM THE TRENCHES: Leaders lead from the front in a Lean transformation

ICICI Bank

The journey of Lean at ICICI Bank began with the implementation of 5S in the early 2000s.

ICICI Bank is the first services company in the world to have deployed 5S enterprise-wide, across all its businesses and companies. The rollout was conceptualized and catalyzed by me and, like all change initiatives, saw many challenges. However, the leadership provided by the then-MD and CEO of ICICI Bank, K.V. Kamath, made all the difference. He personally exhorted the entire top management and employees of the ICICI Group to adopt

(*Continued*)

this simple practice for workplace improvement. And he did not just do the talking. He walked the talk by making sure that the workplace organization through 5S was done first in his office.

The adoption of 5S resulted in:

- Reduction in customer query resolution times,
- Improvement in customer satisfaction scores,
- Enhancement of branch look and feel,
- Productivity improvement,
- Space getting released,
- Documents being retrieved within 30 seconds,
- Employees getting involved in suggestions and workplace improvement.

The success at ICICI Bank and its group companies saw a large number of banks adopting my approach to 5S deployment. Financial services companies who currently practice 5S include HDFC Bank, SBI Life and ING Vyasa, among others.

The blueprint for 5S deployment I created is today a globally accepted practice. The details can be found in my book titled: *5S for Service Organizations and Offices: A Lean Look at Improvement* (ASQ Press, USA, 2006).

Lesson 14

Explain Why We Do What We Do

Implementing Lean is about driving a fundamental change in the way organizations operate. As with all change initiatives it is imperative that we communicate to all concerned the reasons and benefits of implementing Lean. Everyone in the company should know the larger intent and objective which is driving this transformation. A joint team with representatives from top management, middle management and front-liners should take ownership to communicate the following half-dozen questions to everyone in the organization:

1. What is Lean?
2. Why is there a need to adopt Lean now?
3. How does Lean thinking contribute towards achieving the larger vision of the organization?

4. What are the key business objectives that we plan to accomplish through Lean?
5. How would it benefit each one of us?
6. How can each one of us (employees) contribute in the transformation?

Remember, this is not an easy task, especially if the organization is large and scattered across geographies. Someone from the senior management team must take ownership of making this happen. Each of these communication meetings should also be attended by constituents from top management, middle management and front-liners; if there is a union, the representative from the union should also be a part of these meetings. This means that before starting the communication exercise, the management should have a complete alignment with union leaders.

However, it is important to remember that awareness without immediate action is of no use. If there is a long gap between the communication and action, teams can lose sight of what the goal is. It is recommended that the actions on Lean should commence within two weeks of the alignment session.

Figure 2.1 (on the facing page) summarizes the approach to align a proposed Lean transformation with the organization. This begins with the alignment with the board followed by a download to the top management. Both these can be done by the CEO or even an outside facilitator.

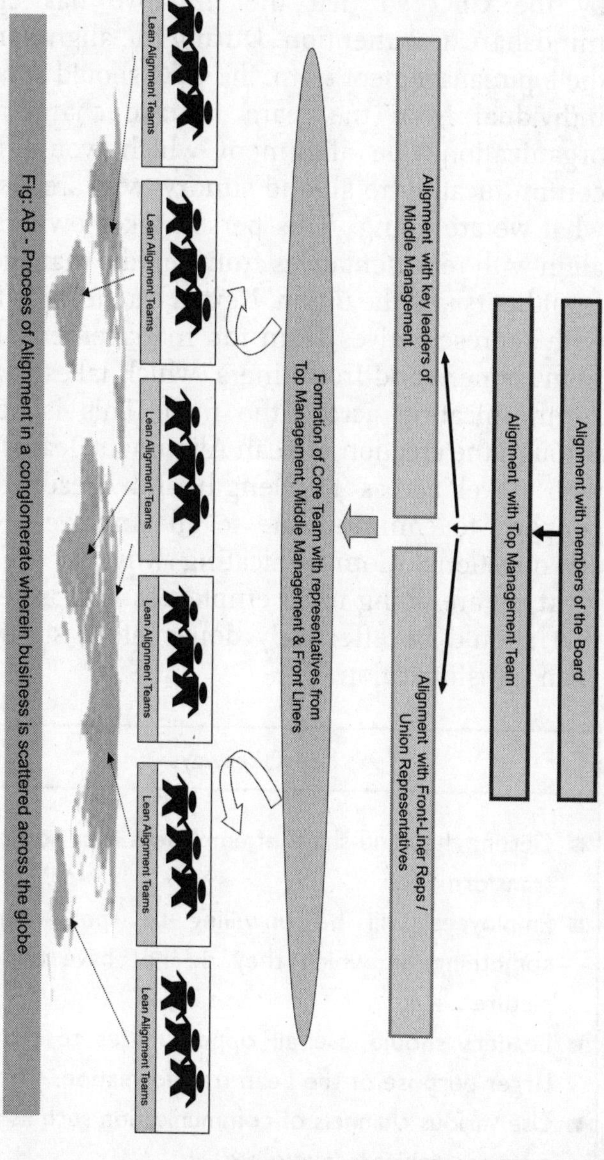

Fig 2.1: Process of Alignment in a Multi-location Global Conglomerate

Sometimes it helps to get an outside resource invited by the CEO so that the initiative has effective mindshare and attention. During the alignment with the top management team, the CEO should appoint an individual from the team to take charge of the organization-wide alignment which would involve communicating to all and sundry 'why are we doing what we are doing'. This person takes ownership to align with representatives from middle management, front-liners and the union. Next, a core team is formed with representatives from top management, middle management and front-liners, which takes charge of communicating across the firm. This is achieved through the creation of Lean Alignment Teams (LATs) who travel across the length and breadth of the conpany to communicate to all employees on the six questions. Communicating why we are doing what we are doing to all employees is a prerequisite that should be effectively done before starting the Lean transformation.

Key Takeaways

- Getting the mind-share of employees is critical to Lean transformation.
- Employees will be unwilling to spend time on something on which they do not have the larger picture.
- Leaders should use all opportunities to share the larger purpose of the Lean transformation.
- Use various channels of communication such as videos, posters, webinars, audio etc.

Lesson 15

Create Interest So Your Team Appreciates the Power of Lean

So, you have decided to commence Lean implementation.

As the Chief Improvement Officer or the Lean Leader, you believe that it is beneficial to your organization. Given the state that your organization is in, you are convinced that Lean is an antidote to many problems. You also know that adopting the practice will take your company to the next level. But what is bothering you is how to get the necessary engagement of the management. You are also a bit skeptical that it may not get the required attention of your colleagues. You know very well that the front-liners may not really come on board till they have seen the benefits. Alternatively, as the CEO, you are convinced of Lean's power. You believe that it is the way forward for competitiveness. However, you would not like to initiate it through a mandate. You would like teams to see the benefit and adopt it.

The first step, even before you make a holistic roadmap, is to create interest in your teams so that they start appreciating what Lean is all about. These are a few things which may create interest in your team members:

- Make your key colleagues and leaders attend a five-day Lean breakthrough public program – This will clearly show them the power of Lean and what a project can deliver in a short period of time. There are consulting companies who hold such experiential workshops.
- Arrange visits to companies who have successfully implemented Lean – There may not be many service-sector companies who have successfully implemented Lean as a business strategy. However, there are a large number of Lean thinking manufacturing companies today. You can learn a lot from them.
- Let representatives from companies who have implemented Lean come and make a presentation in your company. Focus specifically on the success stories.
- Get a Lean thought leader to address the employees of the organization.
- Send a few team members for a value-stream mapping workshop and after they return, make them use it on a process which you believe has inefficiencies.
- Begin with 5S implementation in a few workplaces. This is probably the simplest and best way to get quick results with the involvement

of teams. A successful pilot can create a lot of interest within the organization. (Some details of 5S implementation in a services context have been discussed in Lesson 13). I have successfully led implementation in a large services company and seen what it can do to a non-manufacturing company.

- Take a core process of the organization and Lean it. This would be a pilot to showcase the benefits to the entire organization. Sometimes taking a core process may be difficult, so go for a process wherein there are problems of productivity, lead time, rejections and so on.
- Circulate stories and articles on what Lean has done to organizations. But make sure that they are from reliable sources.

Let me tell you that there is no single solution to make your teams appreciate Lean. It could be a mix of the above strategies. Once you see that a few teams appreciate what Lean can deliver we can create a roadmap. Of course, if you're the CEO this could be relatively easy. However, if you are a Lean change agent you have to get the attention of the CEO or someone in the top management team who can then influence the other members of the leadership.

Once some interest has been created, go ahead and formally launch Lean in the organization. But do not wait for too long to create this interest. One should try and achieve the initial interest creation within a maximum period of six months.

Key Takeaways

- Creating some sort of interest in Lean is a must before formally launching it.
- Building a powerful coalition is a must in the early days of Lean transformation.
- Focus on both the top management and middle-management while creating interest in Lean.
- While targeting middle management only focus on those individuals who have a standing in the firm.
- Do not forget to involve the CFO in the early engagement process.

Lesson 16

Encourage Teams and Individuals to Report Problems

I once was facilitating a Lean breakthrough in a process at a back-office of a services company. The shop was run by a lady who was supposed to be very successful in the organization. She had a command-and-control leadership style and believed in a 'no questions asked' style of management. The team members were expected to execute like robots. The processes were threaded with metrics and employee performance was also measured via metrics. Their increments and bonuses were dependent on meeting the metrics as set up by the Operations Head. She took a lot of pride in having created a 'disciplined' workplace where employees carried out all instructions to a tee.

After the Lean breakthrough was done it came out that there were many wastes in the process and that the process efficiency was less than one per cent. When the final presentation of the findings was made to this lady, she blew up. She rebuked the process owner on running a process laced with wasteful activities. Instead of complimenting the team on the wonderful job they had done in identifying inefficiencies which were tacitly hidden in the crevices of the process, she undid their efforts.

This is an example of how a leader can undo the efforts of Lean. Do you think that the people who were involved in the above Lean breakthrough would ever be comfortable with doing a Lean project? They would never ever dare to reveal the wastes which may be impeding the process performance. They would now hesitate to share the problems and deficiencies of the workplace, as nobody wants their efforts to be not respected.

There is a very important lesson to be learnt here. Leaders implementing Lean should work towards creating a culture where their team members come and report their problems. They should encourage their teams to regularly come and share this concerns pertaining to the process, workplace and the business at large. As a matter of fact, leaders should get worried if teams do not come and report problems on a regular basis. Yes, this is the case even if your department is a performer in your organization and its processes are truly outstanding.

An organization implementing Lean should encourage problem reporting and abnormality identification. Leaders have to shun the command-and-control leadership style which kills the messengers of bad news. In such a scenario, teams will never come up with new ideas. This is foundational to problem solving which is so integral to Lean transformation. Let me tell you that a command-and-control leadership style does not work in today's world. You may get some results in a short time but I doubt if it will sustain over a long timeframe. Command-and-control stifles innovation and impedes all bright individuals who want to positively contribute to the company's success. Can we afford this today when product life cycles are becoming shorter and technology has been a force multiplier? With the large number of opportunities available today, an organization will find it difficult to retain these individuals. A command-and-control leadership style also fosters self-protection wherein individuals try to protect themselves from blame, reprimands and criticisms. This is a sheer waste of organizational time and resources that builds avoidable inefficiencies. If leaders are serious about Lean implementation they have to make these fundamental changes or else it will result in a false start.

Remember, when you have an aware workforce problems will get reported. This is the best thing that can happen to a company. It is always better to report the problems rather than letting them hide in the organizational crevices only to create bigger problems in the future. Let the message go around the firm that problem reporting is a way of life. Train all your employees on problem-solving skills so that they not only report problems but also get involved in solving them. If they are not able to solve them, they should feel free to seek help from others.

Key Takeaways

- Reward employees for reporting problems in the workplace.
- Making employees report problems requires a fundamental culture change in the organization.
- Problems include abnormalities which may not really seem to be problematic today but have the potential to expand to a large issue later.
- A leader should get worried if problems do not get reported on a daily basis.
- Keep an eye on whether the problems recur as it indicates that they are not being solved completely.

FROM THE TRENCHES: Install a live visual board after every process transformation

One of the things that should be done at every location where you do a Lean project is to make use of the Workplace Visual Board. This serves as the information centre used to showcase all the work that the teams do as a part of Lean deployment.

The workplace visual board should have both dynamic and static information. Static information is that which does not change over a period of time. Only 25 per cent of the information on the workplace visual board should be static.

(*Continued*)

The typical items on such a board are:

- Before/After pictures,
- Trends of performance metrics,
- Customer feedback,
- Master index (for storage),
- Problems reported by employees,
- Rules/Policies (related to workplace organization),
- Details about rewards and recognitions.

The workplace visual board (soft-board) should be large enough to be visible to everyone in the workplace. Make a schedule for updating the workplace visual board on an ongoing basis. The information in the workplace visual board should be contextual and interesting. When there is a struggle to get information for display on the workplace visual board, it is an indication that there are challenges in Lean implementation.

CHAPTER 17

LEAN IS MORE THAN JUST TOOLS

I would like to caution all Lean change agents keen on driving Lean: Do not declare early victory. Simply doing a few Lean projects does not mean that Lean has become a part of the organizational fabric. There are many areas where resistance to Lean thinking can occur, but they fall into two broad types. This has been summarized in Table 2.1.

Table 2.1: Active and Passive Resistance

Active Resistance	Passive Resistance
These are resistances about which teams are very vocal and readily share all their concerns. These resistances are easy to manage as one can exactly address the concerns of the impacted employees.	There are quite a few resistances about which teams do not share. They happen by inertia wherein the teams do not adopt what is being pushed. Since they do not share their concerns, it becomes very difficult to address such resistance. Passive resistance can quietly derail the whole movement and the Lean change agents need to be sensitive to this. Proactive efforts have to be made to bring hidden concerns which teams may share about Lean implementation.

Table 2.2 summarizes in greater detail how simply commencing Lean might not deliver benefits to the fullest due to these resistances. As a person driving Lean, one needs to be careful not to land up in such a situation. These are real life cases which I have experienced.

Table 2.2: Challenges to Making Lean an Integral Part of Organizational Fabric

Name	Details
The Dissonance at the Peak (Figure 2.2)	This refers to a state wherein the top management does not have its mind in Lean implementation. The Chief Improvement Officer or Lean leader pushes a Lean agenda but the CEO and his direct reportees do not support it to the fullest. The CEO may give a patient hearing but does not spend time subsequently to get the agenda moving or encourage his reportees to adopt this practice.
The Disonance Midway (Figure 2.2)	This refers to a state wherein engagement is confined to the top management and teams at the grassroots. The middle management is unknowingly kept out or is only partially engaged in the implementation of Lean. Also, this occurs when middle management has limited incentive to adapt to this practice.
The Dissonance at the Foothills (Figure 2.2)	This refers to a state wherein there is little or no engagement amongst the teams in the front-line. There is a lot of hullaballoo and tall claims by the leaders but the teams below are not involved in the transformation. Large projects involve the top and middle management but teams below are not involved. The leaders often look at process associates as robots who have to keep their mouth shut and work.
The Siloed Drive (Figure 2.2)	In this case, the implementation of Lean is confined to a few functions and departments. However, the overall organization does not reap the benefits as the processes improved are not end-to-end and employee engagement does not have a critical mass.

Table 2.2: Challenges to Making Lean an Integral Part of Organizational Fabric

Name	Details
The Lost Ground	This happens when implementation is done but over time the results wane. The leadership team gets aligned, a large number of improvement projects are done, awareness sessions are held for the employees but over a period the benefits recede. The key reason is a lack of infrastructure for sustaining gains.
The Quiet Onslaught	This happens when there is an eerie silence among all the employees across hierarchies (especially middle management and front-liners). The employees are indifferent to the Lean adoption as they believe that it is another 'flavour-of-the-month' initiatives which will come and go. There is skepticism amongst the employees because of their past experiences with similar initiatives which had not led to a logical closure. This also happens when employees think that implementing Lean will lead to the loss of jobs.

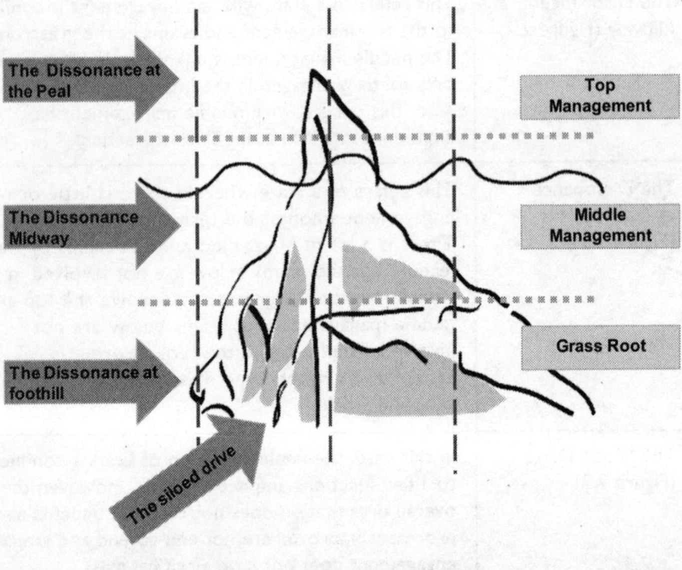

Fig 2.2: Taxonomy of Resistance within Organizations.

Lean thinking, by its very nature has to be practiced day in and day out by everyone in the company. The author has known a senior business leader who was quite effusive about what they had done in Lean implementation, and claimed that his organization would become the Toyota of health-care services. However, it was discovered that they had only done a few Lean breakthrough projects in one of the functions which had given encouraging results. Well, this was a case of declaring early victory before Lean was adopted by the entire organization.

This is a problem with many companies. Just adopting a few tools from the Lean quiver does not make a company a Lean organization. It has to be an all-pervasive initiative that touches everyone in the company across geographies, functions and hierarchies. Like all change initiatives, Lean implementation is not easy, requiring patience and a be-at-it mindset. It has to morph into an enterprise-wide engagement. This happens when adoption enmeshes with practice. This is best summarized in Figure 2.3.

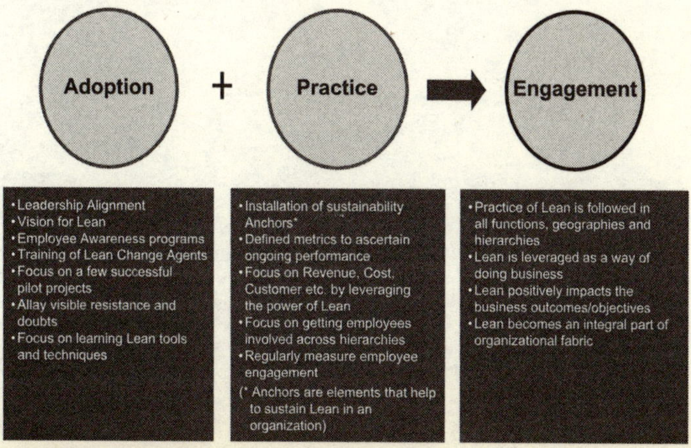

Fig 2.3: Adoption to Engagement: The Lean Approach

Key Takeaways

- Lean Adoption + Lean Practice = Lean Engagement.
- Do not be satisfied with mere Lean adoption; your target should be Lean engagement.
- Ferret out both active and passive resistances to the Lean journey. The latter can be quite difficult to fathom.
- Remember, resistance can manifest in all levels of the organization.

Lesson 18

Employee Attrition is a Major Cause of Inefficiency

One of the biggest hidden inefficiencies in companies is when individuals get recruited but do not stay for long. Money is spent on training/inducting people, only to lose them later. It not only leads to heavy rework but also to a great deal of resource wastage. To my astonishment, some leaders say that attrition is a reality and we need to work our business around it. They rationalize this problem by making the following statements:

- Attrition is an industry-wide phenomenon and we have to live with it.
- Attrition is a problem of an emerging-market wherein the growth of the economy has created plenty of job opportunities.
- Attrition has only been at the grassroots level. There has been no attrition in the leadership team.

- In today's context, you cannot expect a newcomer to stay in an organization more than a year or two.
- This is a Gen-Y problem.
- Beyond a point I do not worry about attrition. I need to just ensure that my diamonds (top-performers) stay in the organization.
- We have been a great training ground. Our colleagues get picked up by the competition.

All the above are manifestations of an 'un-Lean' mindset. Instead of allowing the problems to surface, these individuals are assuming they should not be worried. Further, they go ahead and actually budget for these attritions – a typical 'just-in-case' mindset.

Have you ever wondered why there is employee attrition? More often than not it is because the recruitment process does not have due importance. It is treated as just another HR process. It is defined but only partially and the ideals are not adhered to. Recruitment is not treated as a strategic function in the company.

I was shocked when a business leader during a discussion on Lean implementation mentioned that he needed a few 'working hands' to make Lean a reality in his business. This mindset of treating employees as 'working hands' or robots who will just take instructions and execute them is simply amazing.

Getting the right team set up is probably the first step towards creating a Lean organization. Remember, motivated employees will not only provide great service to customers but also create a great Lean thinking organization.

Many times, the right people do come on board but leave because of the environment provided by the organization. They may not be fully engaged in the endeavours of the company. There could be concerns about the manner in which the leaders treat their employees. The employees may not have a sense of belonging toward the firm and they may be feeling devalued. They may not be used to their full potential and unable to see where their career is moving. They may have stopped learning and adding value to themselves. They may not be having leaders around them whom they can look up to.

So what are the things an organization should do to arrest attrition and ensure that the right individuals come on board?

- Be clear on the type of individuals who you would like to hire both in terms of technical as well as adaptive skills.
- Focus more on attitude than on technical skills. Sometimes companies implementing Lean focus more on whether the individual knows relevant tools and techniques. Remember, you can always train them on Lean tools but if you do not get the right mindset, the game is lost.
- Ensure that the candidates have competencies which meet both short-term and long-term goals. This means that they should not only meet the current requirements but have the skills or potential to grow into future roles.
- Relentlessly communicate to the outside world about the type of talent you are seeking.

- Install a rigorous hiring process – and despite all the pressures, never take short-cuts.
- During the interview probe to discover the behaviour the candidate has demonstrated in the past.
- The candidate should manifest team adding skills or traits.
- Never paint an inaccurately rosy picture during the interview-process – clearly communicate the opportunities, expectations and challenges of the job.
- Look for candidates who are good at problem solving skills, have humility and respect for other people's work/contributions.
- Only hire those individuals who meet the desired values of the firm. Shun the thought that there is a talent shortage and you should hire whoever applies.
- All new inductees should go through a solid foundational training comprising not just functional skills but also information about the company and its values, beliefs and culture.
- Make the performance management system of supervisors accountable for retaining, nurturing and developing talent.

My advice to companies is to draw value-stream maps for the entire recruitment process which include attracting talent, the hiring process, on-boarding process and the first ninety days in the organization. This will clearly bring out the activities which do not add value, such as those which do not help in the development and growth of the new recruit. Make this value-stream map for all key roles in the organization. Remember, the output of this value stream is to get the right quality and quantity of talent, have timely recruitment, and the induction of new recruits in time.

Key Takeaways
■ Not being able to retain the right employees can be a major cause of concern. ■ Treat recruitment as a strategic process of the company. ■ Invest time in getting the right candidate on board. ■ Hire those who align with the values, beliefs and culture of the organization. ■ People are assets whose value appreciates over a period of time. Attract, retain, engage and nurture the right talent and they shall pay huge dividends to the organization.

CHAPTER 19

BUILD A CULTURE OF PROCESS THINKING

Instilling the philosophy of process thinking can be quite a nightmare for organizations. I have seen companies fumble to get it right. This is just not because it is difficult to implement but because leaders do not seem to comprehend what it means to the company and its employees.

Installing process thinking in the company entails instilling the following beliefs among all employees:

- All work is a process.
- Organizational outcomes come through processes.
- Look at all work from a customer's perspective.
- Instead of holding people responsible for problems, find out the processes which cause them.

- Great processes do not require top talent to run them.
- Uncover all influences that break process delivery.

So how does one go about institutionalizing process thinking in an organization?

Educate all your employees across hierarchies on value-steam mapping. If value streaming appears difficult, teach all employees process mapping. While discussing the issues and outcomes of the business, always look at it from a process perspective. This means that if teams or individuals come up with a problem/issue, tell them to list the processes which may be behind the issues and could be impacting it. If there are specific business goals to be achieved, list the processes which help in achieving them. When discussing a sales target, let the sales colleagues list the processes which help in achieving it. Make teams draw process maps for all issues that come up for discussion.

However, this will not just happen. Leaders will have to demand this of the team members. Leaders will have to jettison the mindset of 'first getting results at all costs'.

The second thing that organizations should ask is what impact the processes and activities they run have on the end consumer. If individuals are working on a process, then they should understand what objectives they are trying to accomplish. Who is the customer of the process? Is the focus towards meeting the goals of the department or the requirements of the end-consumer? Move beyond functional silos and put customers and processes at the centre of all organizational activities.

Remember, driving process thinking is not easy. Managers and leaders need to continually communicate the overarching purpose of the process and in early days demand the process connection for all the activities. However, people need to remember that whenever individuals/teams come with a problem, they should query the process behind it (Figure 2.4).

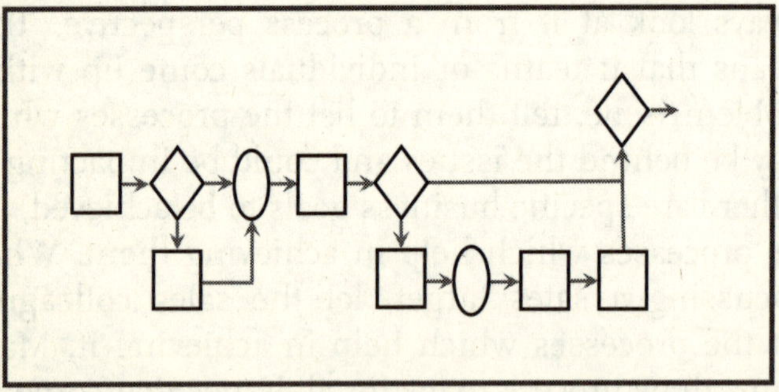

Fig 2.4: What's the Problem? Ask the process!

Key Takeaways
■ Educate all your employees both on value-stream and process mapping. ■ All process associates should be in a position to appreciate their impact on process outcomes. ■ For all business solutions, tell employees in your company to go and ask about the process.

Lesson 20

Resources are Wasted when Employees do not know what Service Means to Them

Whether it is a manufacturing company or service company, 'service' is an integral part of customer delivery. But if you ask a cross-section of employees on what service means to them, you will find that they come up with different responses or may even just give a blank look. In my experience, this is a problem plaguing many companies. In a service organization, employees not knowing what service means to them indicates the need to re-evaluate the service strategy of the organization. It is a symptom of a deep-rooted malady facing the company and a manifestation of leadership not taking 'service' as a key business proposition. You may be wondering how Lean is related to this. We do not realize it, but a lot of resources are wasted because of such a fundamental gap in definition.

Actually it is quite simple: when your employees do not know what service stands for, how do you expect them to provide consistent service? This not only impacts customer satisfaction but confuses the customers about where the organization stands as far as service is concerned. A large amount of employee bandwidth gets lost instead of delivering better customer engagement. This is a huge waste, which could have been avoided by better strategic alignment. If you do a root–cause analysis you shall find the following key reasons for these delivery dissonances:

- Not having a well-defined service intent which defines what constitutes a service experience,
- Gap between the brand personality and customer experience,
- Customers not engaged on what to expect from the company,
- Employees not trained on what should be expected of them.

So, how does one arrest this problem?

This begins with the top management deciding that service will be a strategic thrust of the company.

The deployment of the service strategy begins with the creation of the service-intent, that is, what service means to the company and how this can be disseminated deep and wide within the company and even to the customer.

This brings us to the second point: the strategic service intent, which states the experience that a customer can expect of a firm. This should resonate in every interaction that the organization has with the customer. The strategic service intent is driven by the brand values which the organization defines for itself. All employees who interact with customers have to demonstrate the brand's personality through customer experience. The brand is a promise made to the customer which aggregates as a collection of perceptions in the customer's mind. It is the brand which shapes the expectations of the customers. So it is imperative that there should be consistency between what the brand stands for and what gets delivered by employees who come in contact with customers.

Table 2.3 shows an approach which companies can follow to instill the same understanding of service among all employees:

Table 2.3: Approach to Service Intent Deployment

Step	Details
Delineate Service Intent	This details how the organization would like to treat its customers. What should a customer expect when it experiences the company, its employees or products/services? The service intent should clearly state what the customer can expect from the company and also tell the employees what is expected of them to meet customer expectations.
Reposition Brand Values	The company develops a brand image to embed service dimensions of customer delivery. The brand should reflect the service personality which the company stands for.
Communicate to Employees	The company communicates to all its employees the service promise that it has created for the customer. It also seeks inputs from the employees on the proposed service promise. Employee involvement is the key to making them feel that they are a part of the development process.

Table 2.3: Approach to Service Intent Deployment (*Continued*)

Step	Details
Redefine Roles	Ensure that all employees dealing directly or indirectly with customers spend adequate time in meeting the service promise.
Create Service Standard	Build a solid standard for all points wherein the customer comes in contact with the company. These are activities required to meet the customer's requirements. The endeavour should be to install an engaging experience at each stage of the customer's interaction with your company. These standards help the service intent to become a reality.
Train, Train and Train	Deliver role-specific training programs to employees. Focus on programs which instill service aptitude and develop people skills. Run regular refresher programs to keep teams updated. There should be an equal mix of technical and soft skills in the training programs.
Implement	Implement processes that will work towards supporting and meeting the service intent.
Measure	Track the progress and measure the experience of customers with the company. This could be done through various metrics and audits.

One thing that should be kept in mind: a superlative service delivery requires committed and engaged staff who are kept motivated with a culture that rewards great service performance. Last but not the least, the top management has to treat service as a strategic imperative and competitive differentiator, and not just indulge in lip-service.

Key Takeaways
■ Impeccable service is something which your competitors will find difficult to copy. ■ Without a common definition of what constitutes a service, employees will use their own individual interpretations, with the customer being affected. ■ Make sure that your brand embeds the service dimension of your customer delivery. ■ Not having a holistic service strategy is a major reason for inept customer service. ■ Involve your employees in firming up your service intent.

CHAPTER 21

Continually Create a Sense of Urgency

Merely deciding to embark on a Lean journey is not sufficient. You have to create and communicate to all concerned the necessity of such a step. Creating a sense of urgency can leverage this.

Creating a sense of urgency is about communicating the importance of Lean as the basis for business improvements to all involved. It is about sharing the cost of maintaining the status quo and the impact it will have on the company. The endeavour should be to paint such a picture that it creates concern not only in the leadership but also the teams below, convincing them that change is a prerequisite for survival of the business. Go to the extent of telling them how this will impact them or their work professionaly. This should motivate them to take immediate action. But remember, the change has to be rooted in something which is real and of operational need. It cannot be something abstract and esoteric. Make sure that the business case of the Lean transformation is communicated to the employees in a context that is relevant and understandable to them.

As Lou Gerstner mentioned in his book, *Who Says Elephants Can't Dance?* (2002), 'The sine qua non of any successful transformation is public acknowledgement of the existence of a crisis'. Communicating a sense of urgency helps to overcome overt resistance and is about assuring employees that they would not be blamed about their past work. Leaders at all levels have to demonstrate a sense of urgency for getting things done. They should be in a position to create images of the future after the transformation in the minds of the employees. Tell everyone about the TINA (There Is No Alternative) factor. The compelling message has to be: Change or Perish.

You must be wondering that if business is hunky dory and the leadership is committed then why is there a need to create a sense of urgency. Well, this is required to ensure that all the goals set out under Lean transformation are accomplished. Creating a sense of urgency is imperative for driving any business transformation. Even in a highly successful company such as Toyota Motor Company, creating a sense of urgency is a regular phenomenon. In the book: *Extreme Toyota: Radical Contradictions that Drive Success at the World's Best Manufacturer*, authors Emi Osono, Norihiko Shimizu and Hirotaka Takeuchi write:

> "You have to put your life on the line in order to make something good," said Watanabe[5] a few months after becoming president. "If you compromise in the process, nothing good will come of it. If you listen to this person's and that person's opinion, your spiky horns get dull." He is going to extremes in suggesting that employees put their lives on the line or keep their horns sharpened, but such remarks resonate within the organization. Watanabe seizes every opportunity to instill an atmosphere of urgency. When a string of recalls put a dent in Toyota's reputation for quality during 2006, he made several public apologies and described the problems as a "crisis". Toyota used the quality issue to shake up the whole organization, its subsidiaries and its suppliers.

The current CEO of Toyota, Aiko Toyoda, also created the same sense of urgency to shake up the organization from late 2009 to 2011, and a new Toyota Motor Corporation is emerging from this. You may be the best performing company but remember only those who are paranoid about the status-quo can survive.

The following is a list of must dos which are required for creating a sense of urgency before you start Lean transformation efforts:

- Make sure that the message is sincere and does not look contrived and fake.
- At least 80 per cent of the leadership team (the CEO and direct reports) should believe that there

[5] Katsuaki Watanabe was the president and CEO of Toyota Motor Corporation from June 2005 till June 2009.

is a crisis-like situation and the Lean journey is a must for survival.

- Use all available opportunities to communicate the importance of and urgency for Lean adoption.
- Communicate to the entire organization the core reasons which are driving it to adopt Lean.
- Share all facts so that the employees clearly know the reason for the change.
- Use various channels to communicate the need for change such as town-hall meetings, presentations by executives, posters, metrics and targets.
- Achieve a critical mass of employees who will lead the change through Lean – 30 per cent of your employees should be in this segment.
- Try to stir the emotions of the employees so that they can be convinced.
- Shun the know-it-all mindset. If you see this in your employees, the CEO and other leaders should break the backbone of this mindset.

Remember, just creating a sense of urgency once during the start of the Lean journey is not sufficient. It has to done again and again. Lean transformation has to be anchored on a solid business case but driven by emotions.

Key Takeaways

- Before starting Lean implementation share with teams the reasons that are driving this movement.
- Leaders should take every opportunity to share the urgency for Lean transformation.
- If your employees do not see the urgency, they will not commit to carrying out the change.
- Do not over-communicate the sense of urgency—it can fill employees with emotions such as anger, worry, dejection or panic.

CHAPTER 22

ENSURE THAT MIDDLE MANAGEMENT IS FULLY ENGAGED

In a Lean transformation, special attention should be given to ensure that the middle management is taken on board adequately. This is required because the middle management often does not get complete attention.

Organizations spend a lot of time engaging the leadership team by conducting alignment workshops and preparing for them as a part of management reviews. Teams on the shop floor, individuals working on process and front-liners are taken through awareness programs and encouraged to take up projects. However, little attention is paid to engage the middle management. The lack of attention makes middle-management employees disinterested in the transformation. The thought that bothers them is: why should we be a part of a movement which has been launched without involving us? What further bothers them is that it would increase their workload. In an article titled 'Who Wants to be a Middle Manager?' published in *USA Today*, author Stephanie Armour writes:

> Middle-management jobs have become more demanding. Technology means middle managers have to do more multitasking and are expected to be accessible to their staffs, a Herculean challenge in the age of globalization. Employees may be spread across the globe, and a manager may have to get up at 3 a.m. to take a call from an employee in another country.

The feeling that bothers them is that this is another of those flavour-of-the-month type of initiatives which come and go. Given these challenges, getting middle management on board requires extra effort and requires the senior management's attention. Remember: a middle management with partial mind-share results in a stillborn engagement (Ref: Figure 2.2).

In today's world, when the shelf-life of Chief Executive Officers has reduced, full engagement of the middle management is a must for sustaining the gains from Lean. As a matter of fact, one of the true indications of successful Lean transformation is when the middle management engages in driving and making the Lean transformation work. The top management will set the vision but it is the middle management that makes it happen. They will communicate with people on the grassroots and frontline on the impact of change. It is imperative that a program be designed within the larger transformation agenda to engage the middle management and here are some of the must-dos:

- An alignment session with the middle management, specifying the relevance of Lean and how it would create a high performance business.
- Make each person in middle management learn how to appreciate and identify waste.
- Familiarize middle management with both the strategic and tactical aspects of Lean.
- Look for individuals with high influencing abilities and passion for change. Give them ownership to drive Lean in their respective work-areas.
- Give ownership of a few critical projects to leaders in middle management. However, these projects should have the sponsorship of top management or we may lose the link.
- Use middle management as the communicator and translator of management's thought/perspective on the transformation.
- Clearly communicate that this is not just another passing fad.
- Seek the feedback of middle management to design and co-create the various programs in the Lean journey.
- Capture their voices and expectations on their perspective on Lean.
- Top management should regularly ask what support is required.
- Organize visits to companies who have got a good traction on Lean.
- Reward for good performance.
- Clearly differentiate between the compensation of middle management and front-liners.

- Involve them in the change process – the more they come on board, the easier the acceptance and adoption.
- Different people have different concerns – so try and address all senses as possible, and if required apply various modes of communication.

One of the mechanisms is to ascertain the engagement levels of middle managers on a regular basis. Administer the Lean engagement instrument every quarter and establish an engagement index. If you do not see a positive trend in the index, it would mean that something needs to be done or the current engagement process is inadequate.

Remember, middle managers do have a lot of information and directly manage the front-liners. Middle managers are the ones who deploy strategy and help in achieving the short-term goals of the company. You can never progress on a Lean journey without taking them on board.

Key Takeaways
■ The true test of a leader being able to inspire the company on Lean is when the middle management willingly takes action. ■ An engaged middle management is a must for embedding Lean thinking in a company. ■ Ascertain the engagement levels every quarter to have a fix on middle management's mindshare. ■ Familiarize middle management on both the strategic and the tactical aspects of Lean.

Section 3

Process

Process

When we talk about process here, we are referring to the approach adopted for deployment. The focus is not just about 'process' per se which we understand to be a set of activities working in tandem to convert input into an output, but includes all those things required to be done during the execution of a Lean transformation. A key fact of this is process orientation whch is about making sure that the focus is not just on results but also on the process which makes them happen. The right process should be targeted and it has to be managed in an effective manner to get the desired results. Leaders need to continuously drill into the teams that great performance is about getting the desired results by using the right processes.

Remember, employing a great set of people but without reliable processes does not make a company world-class. What makes a company great are dependable processes managed by a team comprising great and average performers. In the latter case, reliable processes make up for the capability gaps in average people.

Lean is about continually getting back to the basics and making sure that they are in order. One of the fundamental basics is the 'standard work procedure'— the best known method of doing a job which has been documented and is available at the point of usage. However, leaders need to make sure that teams adhere to these standard processes/procedures. Standard work does not make employees robots but makes sure teams do not waste time in solving avoidable small issues. The focus for teams should be on problem–solving in the larger sense, which expands the intellectual capacity of individuals.

"If you can't describe
what you are doing as a process,
you don't know what you're doing."

—W. Edwards Deming

Lesson 23

The DEB-LOREX™ Model for Lean Transformation

The implementation of Lean in a service context is about the intelligent customization of tools that have been applied to manufacturing organizations. CEOs often ask if there is a holistic model which will provide them direction on how to go about implementing Lean. My response is The Toyota Production System is the model you should look for. However, if you find it difficult to comprehend as you may not have worked in a service organization, I would recommend that you go for the DEB-LOREX™ model for holistic Lean deployment. The model focuses on elements that are required to make a Lean service organization.

The components that make up the DEB-LOREX^{TM} Management System (Figure 3.1) are as follows:

- Leadership
- Functions
- Value Streams
- Anchors
- Lean Thinking
- Results.

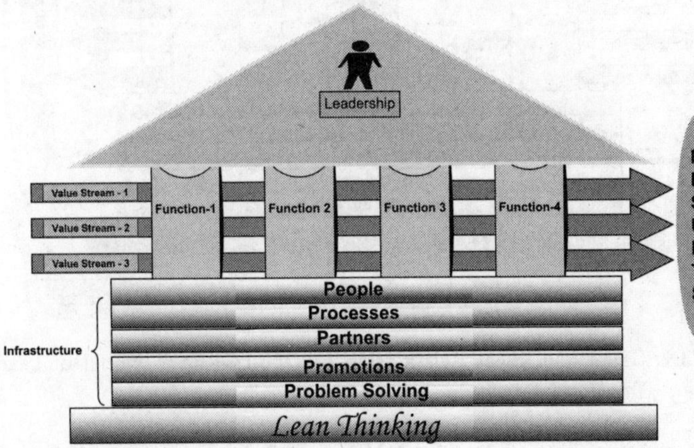

Fig 3.1: DEB-LOREX™ Model for Lean Transformation

For Lean to deliver sustained benefits, it is imperative that all the components of the Lean Management System function in harmony. During Lean transformation, each of the elements of the DEB-LOREX^{TM} management system must be properly implemented. Inadequacies in any of them will impair the overall expected performance of the organization. The first four elements, comprising Leadership, Functions, Value Streams, Lean thinking and Anchors, are the enablers, or causes in the DEBLOREX™ Lean Management System, that make the results happen (Figure 3.2).

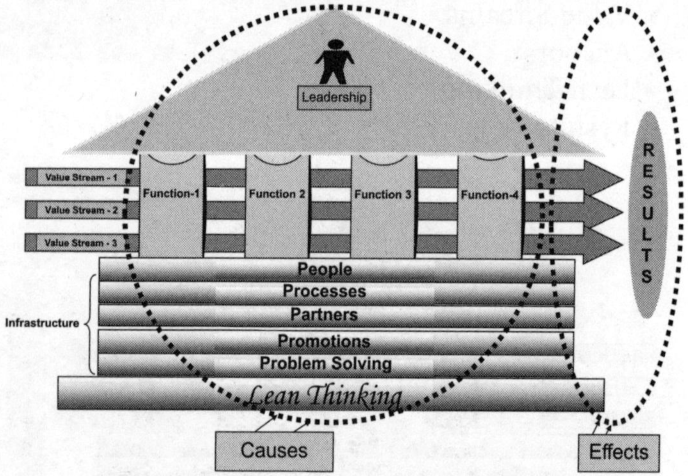

Fig 3.2: Cause and Effect Relationship of DEB-LOREX™ Model of Lean Transformation

The adequacy of each of the enablers/causes will have a direct impact on the performance of the company. For example, an organization may have great processes, but without leadership commitment, it cannot expect the management system to deliver value. As the implementation of Lean matures in the company, leaders will be in a position to clearly say which of the enablers (or causes) need to be acted upon to get the desired results.

Key Takeaways

- The DEB-LOREX™ model provides a handy approach to taking service companies to a new level of efficiency.
- Following a holistic model such as DEB-LOREX™ will ensure that you do not forget any of the critical elements in the Lean journey.
- Without focus on Anchors, a Lean journey can be incomplete.
- Treat Lean as a business strategy for improving a business system, not just a few processes.

Lesson 24

Lead Time and Throughput Time are not the Same

Lean is often called time-based management. This is because one of the prime objectives of Lean is to reduce the lead time of a process. This is the end-to-end time required for execution of a process and starts from the time the customer places the order till the customer receives the product or service.

Practitioners of Lean often commit a mistake and treat *Lead Time* and *Throughput Time* synonymously. Please note that throughput time is the time taken towards execution of a process. It is the time taken to complete a process from start to end. In the manufacturing world throughput time is often called Dock-to-Dock time, which is the amount of time taken from the time material is received till the finished product is shipped to the customer.

By treating throughput time synonymously with lead time, Lean practitioners often overlook a segment of the time involved, as shown in Figure 3.3.

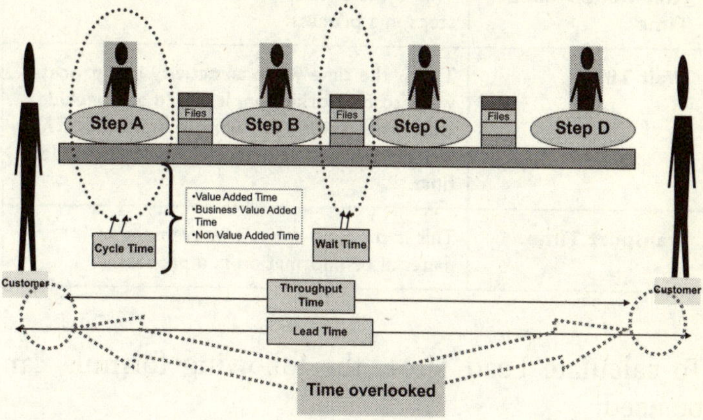

Fig 3.3: Difference between Lead Time and Throughput Time

However, to facilitate improvements through Lean, we need to know much more than the two times discussed above. So, what are the times relevant for Lean in service sector organisations? Table 3.1 lists the various times used in a transactional environment.

Table 3.1: Various Times of Lean

Various Times of Lean	Definition
Cycle Time	This is the time taken to execute an activity in a process. For example, in pre-loan processing, the time taken for verification would be one cycle time.
Value-Added Time	This is the time spent doing value-added activities in a process.
Business-Value-Added Time	This is the time spent on business-value-added steps in a process.

Table 3.2: Various Times of Lean (*Continued*)

Various Times of Lean	Definition
Non-Value-Added Time	This is the time spent on non-value-added steps in a process.
Wait Time	This is the time when an activity in a process waits to be worked on. It would also include individuals waiting for work in a process. This will get included as a part of non-value-added time.
Transport Time	This is the time spent in movement of material or information in a process.

To calculate Lead Time, the following formula can be used:

Lead Time = Value Added Time + Business-Value-Added Time + Non-Value-Added Time

Looking at Figure 3.3, the equation of Lead Time can be modified as shown below:

Lead Time = Cycle Time + Wait Time + Transport Time + Other Non-Value-Added Time

To calculate the throughput time of a process, use the following formula:

$$\text{Throughput Time} = \frac{\text{Average Inventory in the process}}{\text{Rate at which product or service is manufactured}}$$

$$= \frac{\text{Work in Progress (or Things in Progress}^{*}\text{)}}{\text{Average Completion Rate}}$$

(*Raw material, work-in-progress, finished goods)

Please note that Lead time and Throughput Time could be the same in a process. However, sometimes lead time could also be less than throughput time. This is possible when we have been able to pre-ready the goods and services required by the customer. This means that the production of the goods or services has already been done and inventoried. So when a customer seeks the company's services, the item is already ready for purchase/consumption. This reduces the lead time substantially, as it is the time taken to complete a process from the time an order is placed till it's delivered to the customer.

Key Takeaways
■ It is important to understand the various times of Lean such as cycle time, lead time, throughput time, wait time, transport time etc. ■ The lead time of a process can be less than throughput time if the good or service has been inventoried in advance. ■ As a Lean practitioner your focus should be to first reduce the lead time of a process and then focus on the throughput time. ■ Service organizations should seriously think of using self-service as an approach to reduce lead times.

FROM THE TRENCHES: Looking at layout becomes imperative to reduce lead times.

Changing the layout and making it cellular can pay huge dividends during Lean transformation. As in manufacturing, you make pseudo cells which improve the flow of documents and reduce the time needed to serve customers substantially. One thing that is often measured during such a process is the distance travelled by the document during processing. Sometimes it is astonishing to see how slowly documents move, making the customer wait. Figure 3.4 shows via a before-and-after picture the result of a Lean transformation done in the processing shop of a financial services business. As you can see, by using the principles of small batches and loop-back reduction the document's travel-time reduced from 93 feet to 24 feet. The outcomes of the project were that there was an almost 70 per cent reduction in lead time and 80 per cent reduction in errors.

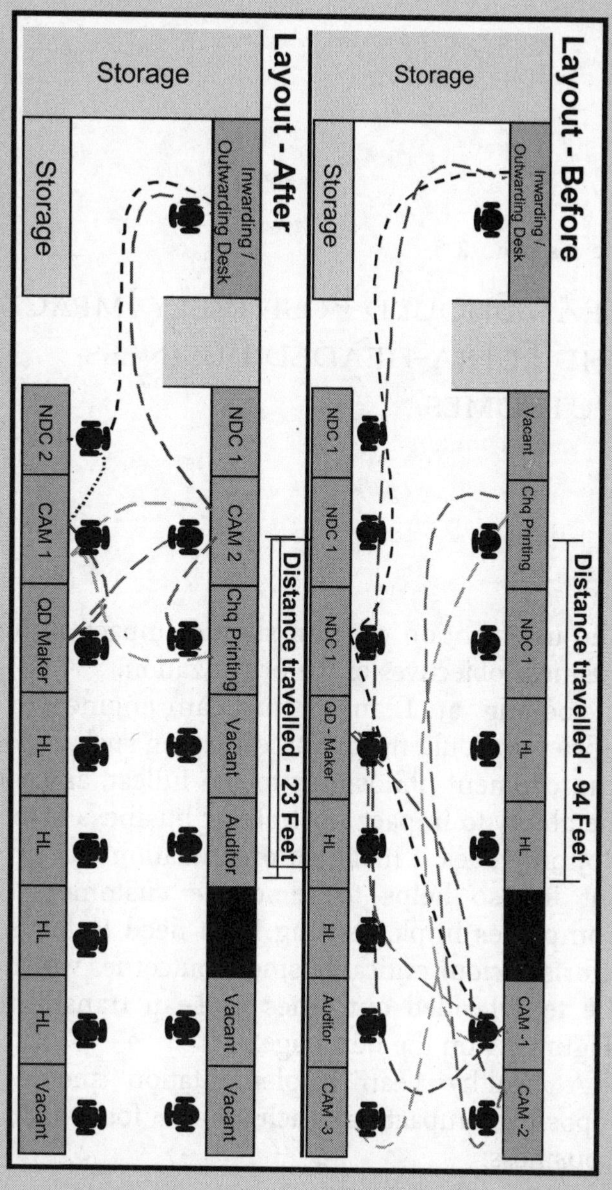

Fig 3.4: Before vs After Picture of a Layout Change after a Lean Event

Lesson 25

Lean Should Positively Impact the Tetra-headed Business Outcomes

The intervention of Lean should impact all the key business objectives of the organization.

Looking at Lean as just an engine for cost efficiency would mean not leveraging such a powerful improvement philosophy to the fullest, as Lean has the ability to impact all strategic business objectives. Not only does it make an organization cost efficient but it also helps to serve the customers better. Companies implementing Lean need to focus their efforts on four critical business outcomes which I call the tetra-headed outcomes of Lean transformation (Figure 3.5 on the next page).

A healthy Lean implementation should have a positive impact on each of the four metrics of a business:

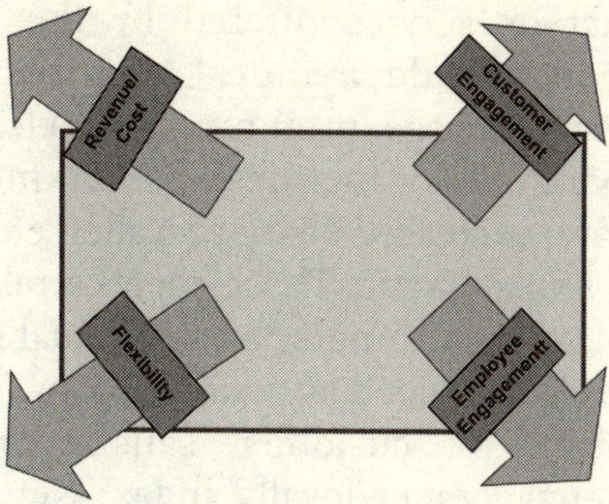

Fig 3.5: The Tetra-Headed Outcomes of Lean

Flexibility: These metrics measure the ability of the organization to cost-effectively meet the varying needs of the customer, marketplace and the ecosystem in which it operates. The marketplace includes visible and invisible current/potential competitions while the ecosystem includes stakeholders such as regulators, shareholders, partners, newer types of risks etc. Examples of flexibility metrics are: the number of exceptions handled, number of new products introduced and number of customized solutions to customers.

Employee Engagement: These look at the level of engagement of members who are directly or indirectly impacted by the Lean transformation. If Lean is being deployed in the entire company, it would include all employees and the change in their level of engagement after deployment. Examples of engagement metrics are people engagement percentage and penetration percentage across hierarchies.

Cost/Revenue: These tell us about the impact of the transformation on the top-line or bottom-line of the company. They also include the impact on the cost of the product or service offered by the company. Cost efficiency could manifest as a reduction in price, a service charge, premium, fees, etc. Revenue enhancement could manifest as an increase in market-share, increased share-of-wallet, etc.

Customer Engagement: These metrics relate to the feedback from customers on the quality of the product/service provided by your company. This could be measured by customer satisfaction scores, customer engagement/loyalty index, Net Promoter Score etc.

The management should regularly monitor the performance of each of the four metrics. A downward trend in any one of the outcomes would mean gaps in implementation and the leadership should find out what is incorrect. Assuming that you are using the DEB-LOREX^{TM} model for your Lean journey, it should positively impact the tetra-headed outcomes of Lean (Figure 3.6).

Does this mean that we shall not be looking at metrics such as quality, lead time, and productivity? No, we shall definitely be doing so, but in terms of the processes. The tetra-headed outcomes are business objectives and are a result of the performance of organizational processes. They are strategic metrices and should not be confused with metrices used to measure process output. The process metrices that get positively impacted by a Lean effort are: lead time, quality (such as error rejections, first pass yield etc) and resource utilization (such as manage owner productivity, material usage etc).

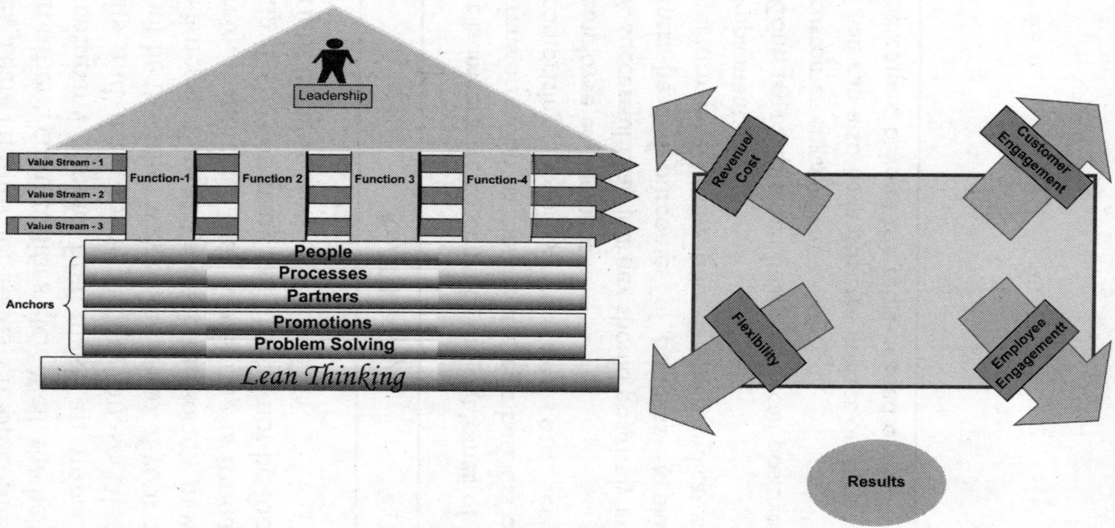

Fig 3.6: The DEB-LOREX™ Model and the Tetra-Headed Outcomes of Lean

Does this mean that the organization which drives Lean should not focus on outcomes around environment, communities etc.? Well, the belief is that the company should first make an impact on the profits and then spend money on social issues. It cannot be the other way round. Also, if your outcomes have a negative impact around the society in which you operate, it indicates that something is fundamentally wrong in the company and it may not be focusing on the right things.

Key Takeaways
■ It is imperative to connect the outcomes of the Lean transformation to the key strategic business objectives comprising flexibility, revenue, cost, service and employee engagement. ■ A successful Lean journey should positively impact the tetra-headed outcomes of business—a plummeting performance in any one of them indicates gaps in implementation. ■ Contrary to common belief, Lean can positively impact customer engagement. ■ Lean can also have positive impact on other business outcomes, beyond the tetra-headed ones.

Lesson 26

Continually Ascertain the Health of Lean

Companies often begin Lean transformations with a big bang, but after some time the deployment loses steam. While derailment is always obvious, it makes sense for one to keep an eye on things that are not happening as desired from the beginning, before they get to the derailment stage. However, this requires deeper insights into the nuances of Lean implementation and the relevant change dimensions around it. This approach can be subjective and person driven. This is where a diagnostic tool as shown in Table 3.2 (on the next page) can be of help.

I would recommend that leaders spend fifteen minutes each quarter to ascertain whether their journey is underway as desired. For large organizations, this tool can be used by leaders in each of the locations/geographies. The tool is so handy that leaders across hierarchies can use it.

Table 3.2 Deb's Lean Health Assessment Tool

Pointers	Yes/No
There is another competing initiative which is being run in the company.	
You see major political resistance (internal or external) which the senior management cannot/or would not like to overcome.	
You see Lean not being driven as a strategy to take the performance of the company to the next level but as another passing fad.	
You do not see members of the top management team taking out time to drive the Lean transformation.	
The required resources have not been provided for the success of this intervention.	
The roll out of Lean is not getting the required visibility in the company.	
The outcomes of Lean are not threaded to the performance management of all key employees in the company.	
Approach to project selection is ad hoc and does not follow a business rationale.	
The initiative is largely being run by the team members of the Lean office without participation of the line teams.	
The measures of success have not been defined clearly.	
Teams are being pushed into projects without proper skill development.	
Teams are branding cost-cutting initiatives as Lean.	
The Lean roll out is happening with a mandate from the top but with no inputs from the employees.	
Implementation of Lean is project-based and there is no focus on the Anchors.	

The Lean health instrument may not be very comprehensive but does give a quick peek into where your deployment is heading. It will let you know the lever that needs to be pressed to get the desired success. Once you have completed the tool, use Table 3.3 for interpreting the results.

Table 3.3: Interpreting Scores from Deb's Lean Health Assessment Tool

Number of "Yes's"	Interpretation
Greater than 7	Major cause of worry. You need to see if you have conceptualized your roll out correctly. It also puts a question mark on your Chief Improvement officer/Lean Leader or the person who is guiding the company on Lean efforts
5–7	It's worrisome. Find the reasons for the gaps.
Less than 5	May not be a cause of great worry but do find out the reasons.

In the early days of the journey, you will never find everything in place. However, with a well thought-out roadmap, you will exactly know when and where the deployment is arrested.

Key Takeaways
■ A fifteen-minute effort to ascertain the health of Lean can go a long way to avoiding untoward surprises about employee engagement. ■ Do not commence Lean implementation if there is another competing initiative underway. ■ The outcomes of Lean should be threaded with the performance management system of all employees.

Lesson 27

Process Ownership is the Key to Enhancing Efficiency

On a manufacturing shop-floor, the processes generally have well-defined owners. These individuals take complete ownership of the process output deliverables and manage all issues pertaining to them.

However, this is often not the case in service organizations. Lack of process ownership results in a large number of inefficiencies, and impacts the overall effectiveness of the process. This is often because of the functional structure of the organizations. While processes flow horizontally, the functions work towards vertical agglomeration. This results in:

- Local optimization: The focus is on meeting the goals within the functions instead of the process goals. This leads to stagnant performance within each of the functional silos, without really impacting the other silos.

- Customers as Orphans: Nobody owns the customer and his or her requirement. Each of the functions focuses on meeting their vertical objectives and the needs of the customer suffer.
- Hand-Off Misses: This refers to misses that happen as the individual silos complete their process activity and pass on the baton to the next silo in the process loop.
- Myopic Measurements: The metrics which get tracked within each of the silos do not give a complete overview of total process performance and how effectively it meets the customer requirements.
- Missed Process Outcomes: The outcome of the total process is not owned by anyone. This results in processes often not meeting their desired results.
- Process dissonance: There is no one to manage the coordination of different processes.

If the company is cast around processes and value-streams, driving process ownership is quite easy. However, it requires structural change in organizations built around functions. This may not always be easy. Carrying out a structural change could actually derail the entire thought as the company may not really be ready to undergo the pain.

This is where you need to discover hybrid approaches which an organization can follow to drive process ownership. Here are some ideas:

- Create a team comprising senior members from each of the functional silos who jointly own the entire process (Figure 3.7). This team should be made responsible for the overall performance of the process. They meet on a regular basis to manage the issues pertaining to cross-functional coordination.

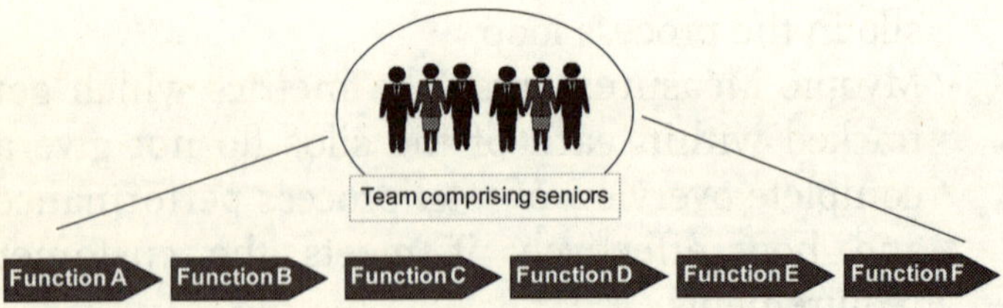

Fig 3.7: Joint ownership of Process by Senior Members of Functions

- Make leaders from the top management team responsible for the core processes of the company. These individuals could be one or two levels below the CEO. They should essentially be in a position to drive the actions of functional leaders towards achieving the larger objectives of the process. This role could be played in rotation but it is important that ownership remains for a period of at least two years (see Figure 3.8).

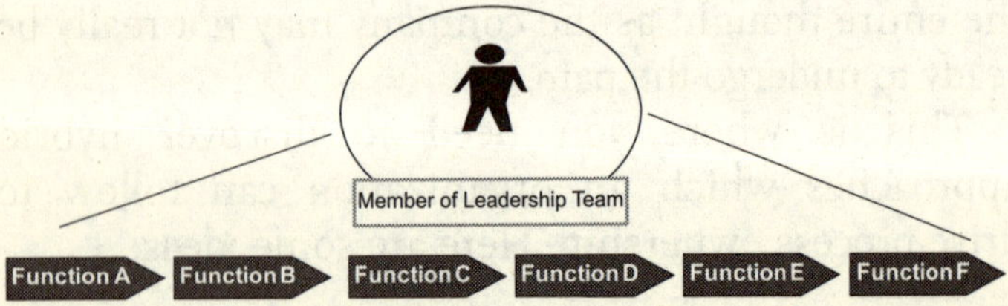

Fig 3.8: Members from the Leadership Team Own the Process

Driving ownership of processes that cut across geographies can be quite arduous. It requires solid leadership and commitment to manage coordination and hand-off issues pertaining to processes. In such a scenario, the process owner has to develop globally-aligned processes that address region-specific needs. Table 3.4 summarizes the key roles of a process owner.

Table 3.4: Role of a Process Owner

1. Takes ownership for overall performance of a process,
2. Owns the customer of the process,
3. Responsible for managing change across the process,
4. Manages interface, hand-off and cross-functional issues,
5. Shares process metrics and monitors performance,
6. Responsible for driving improvements across the process,
7. Ensures process change happens and ascertains the impact of changing functional and geographical capabilities,
8. Identifies best practices that will improve overall process effectiveness,
9. Establishes strategies and priorities for investments in the processes,
10. Helps to integrate people, technology and leadership in a process.

Key Takeaways

- Lack of process ownership is a major cause of process discomforts and the issues related to the process being able to meet the outcome.
- Driving process ownership would require that the top management be willing to change the way the company is structured.

- All value-creating/core processes of the organization must have process ownership.
- Process owners provide stewardship to processes, taking the organization to a new level of performance.

Lesson 28

VALUE STREAM MANAGEMENT IS THE HEART OF LEAN

What is a value stream?

The Lean Lexicon by Chet Marchwinski and John Shook defines a value stream as: 'All of the actions, both value-creating and non-value-creating, required to bring a product from concept to launch and from order to delivery.' It includes all the steps involved in taking a product from conceptualizing till the money comes back to the organization. It comprises broad steps such as concept to launch, order to delivery and order to cash. Remember, the value stream brings together all the steps that comprise a business for a product family, that is, a group of products, which broadly follow the same process steps.

At a conceptual level, a value stream has six blocks, as shown in Figure 3.9 on the next page.

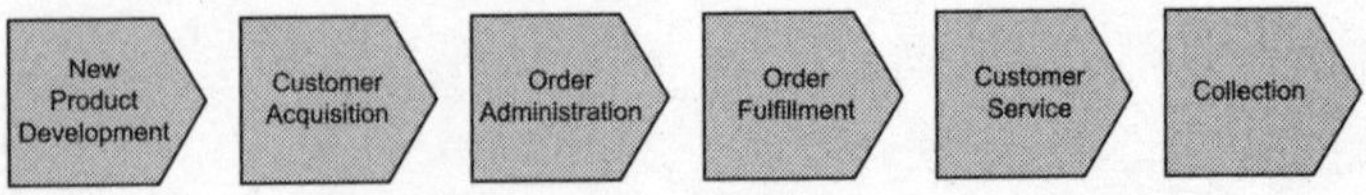

Fig 3.9: Generic Value Stream

Irrespective of the type of products or industry, whether it is a consumer goods or a financial product company, they all follow these generic steps. While there can be a minor change in the sequence, the six blocks of the values stream will always exist in all business units. Figure 3.10 shows the generic value stream of a mortgage finance business.

During Lean deployment, the teams work across these blocks to create efficient processes that deliver superlative performance.

Value streams also have end-to-end process maps within them. These are also called process loops. One of the goals of a Lean transformation is to optimize the performance of process loops within the value streams.

Key Takeaways
■ A value stream comprises all value-adding and non-value-adding activities required to run a business. ■ Value streams are always for a product family. ■ Each value stream has a set of process loops which are to be treated as a strategic asset of the company. ■ Leveraging the value stream for effective delivery is a key objective of Lean transformation.

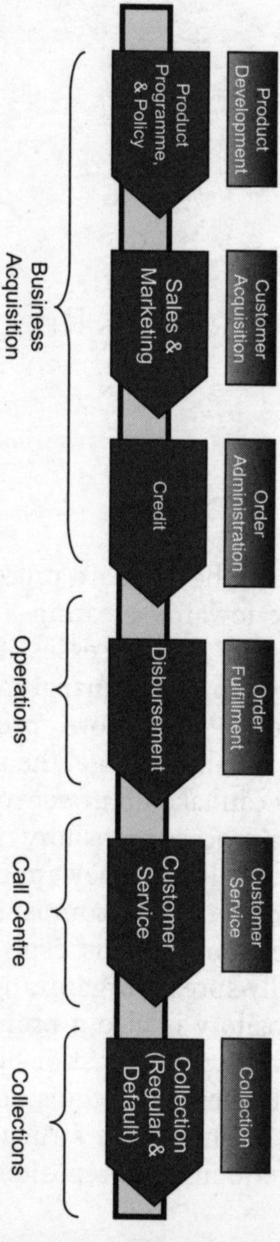

Fig 3.10: Value Stream of a Mortgage Finance Business

Lesson 29

Create a Process Repository

Having defined the standard processes, organizations should work towards creating a holistic repository which stores all the processes in the organization. This not only provides transparency to all concerned, but also helps to remove process complexities. A repository also helps to get the uninitiated on board fast and they can take up newer roles with less hassle.

Creating a process repository must seem like such a no-brainer. Well, this may appear to be something which should be there in companies, but the reality is that it's often not. This is especially true for large geographically-spread organizations. Not having a process repository is also a problem for companies which may have grown fast or been through a large number of mergers and acquisitions.

Figure 3.11 shows the structure that companies should follow to install a repository for processes.

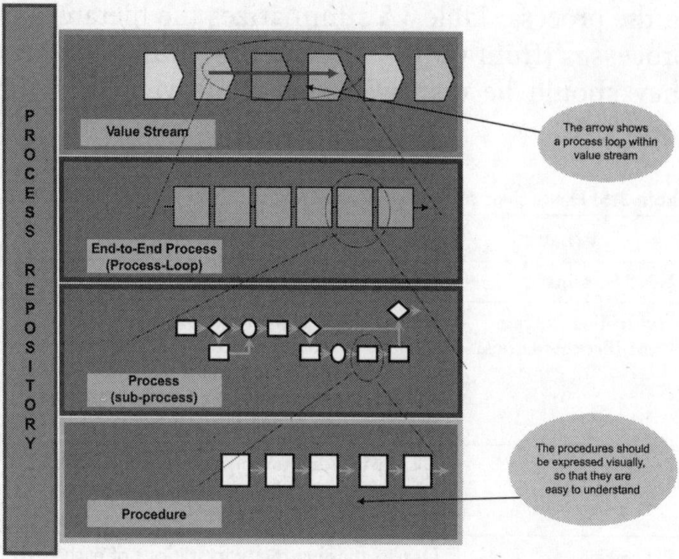

Fig 3.11: Structure of A Process Repository

The repository could either be in an electronic or a physical form. However, in today's technology-centric world it makes sense to create the repository in an electronic form. That way, one does not have the headache of sending newer versions every time a process gets updated and take back copies of the old processes. In an electronic/web-based environment, the user sees the updated processes every time. All the changes to the repository get maintained and controlled by a central process team.

Creating a repository helps employees (process associates) to see the larger picture on how their work impacts the customer. They also get perspective on how their work relates to the work of other associates in the process. Table 3.5 summarizes the hierarchy of processes (from value stream to procedure) and how they should be displayed and made visible in the company.

Table 3.5: Hierarchies of Processes and How to Make Them Visible

What	Where
Value Streams	Display them across the organizations
End-to-End Process Maps (Process Loops)	Display these in workplaces and functions through which the process passes for teams to see who their customers* are, how their work interacts with other functions and the impact on the end-user/consumer**.
Process	Display the relevant processes (sub-processes) in respective workplace/department visual boards
Procedure	Display these in the workstations of each process associate. These should be visual in nature.

* Customers refers to the next team who is the receipent of the work done by this team in the process.

** End user/consumer refers to customers who finally use or consume the product or service made by the process.

To summarize, the benefits of a process repository are as follows:

- Provides a common currency for managing processes in an organization,
- Provides the larger context to associates beyond their isolated works,
- Forces teams to avoid work-around solutions as processes cannot be changed at the drop of a hat,
- Encourages collaboration as teams can see each other's processes,
- Ideal for distributed teams which have a common goal to achieve,
- Increases process compliance and consistency.

Key Takeaways

- A process repository helps to increase the transparency of processes.
- It helps to get new recruits on board without any hassle.
- A process repository is a strategic asset of the company which stores employee experience and expertise.
- A process repository is foundational to a process-thinking organization.

FROM THE TRENCHES:

INFOSYS LTD.

As a service company, Infosys Technologies provides a good example of an effective business process management system. The business process management initiative articulated through PRIDE (Process Repository at Infosys Driving Excellence) provides a number of core capabilities to the organization. The primary objective of PRIDE is to serve as a platform for the mapping of the organization's processes to its business needs. A variety of reports help leaders at all levels in project execution and decision making. This process repository is an industry benchmark and worth emulating. The beauty of PRIDE is that it encapsulates best practices from Infosys locations all over the world and is continuously updated.

Lesson 30

SET UP A LEAN OFFICE

The implementation of Lean requires a central team to manage adoption, deployment and sustain the gains from the transformation. The team entrusted with this job is called the Lean office. This team reports into the Chief Improvement Officer, or Lean leaders, and takes ownership for providing technical support, building change management capabilities and catalyzing the transformation. When you decide to implement Lean in your company, put together a Lean office.

I have seen leaders debunking the need for such an office. Let me tell you, without such a project management office, very soon the implementation will flounder. You will soon see that there is no one to track and measure the implementation.

Have decided to put together a Lean office, you need to ensure that it has the right resources, including the right people in the right roles, so that the Lean office can deliver value to the transformation. Figure 3.12 and Table 3.6 summarize the various types of individuals who should staff the Lean office.

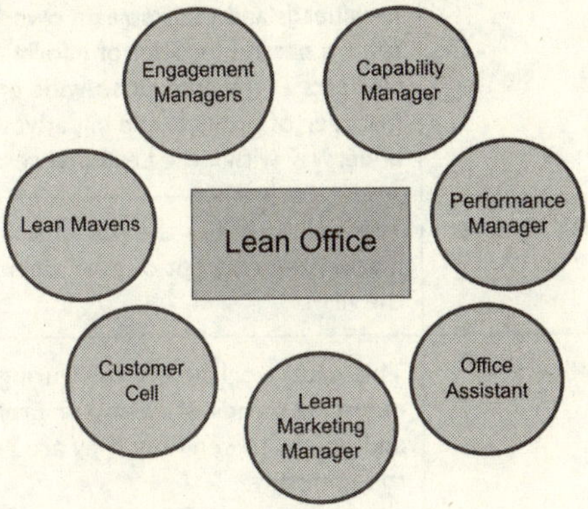

Fig 3.12: The Various Constituents of a Lean Office

Table 3.6: The Composition of a Lean Office

Role	Description
Lean Mavens	These are methodology experts on Lean who provide technical support to the company. They give teams guidelines for their projects.
Engagement Managers	These are individuals who are entrusted with the role of influencing business units and individuals to adopt Lean practices for betterment. They need not be Lean experts but do manage a set of projects. They typically engage with senior leaders and value-stream owners of the company.
Capability Manager	This individual manages capability development activities around Lean in the company. S/he works out the larger capability-building strategy for Lean transformation and ensures that relevant skills are embedded in relevant places. S/he leverages resources from within the Lean office or outside the company to actually deliver the training programme.

Table 3.6: The Composition of a Lean Office (*Continued*)

Role	Description
Performance Manager	This individual manages the performance of Lean transformation. S/he shares performance metrics with the entire organization. The business heads and value stream owners depend on this person for a lot of information. S/he also acts as the enterprise-wide project manager of projects and initiatives that are underway within the Lean umbrella.
Lean Marketing Manager	This individual has the responsibility to market the concept of Lean deep within the firm.
Customer Cell	This team works towards figuring out emerging trends of customer preferences and needs, to see how they are relevant to the company.
Office Assistant	This individual manages the Lean office and makes presentations for the engagement managers and Lean mavens. S/he also carries out the administrative activities of the Lean office.

These people play the key roles of the Lean office, namely[3]:

- Scripting the organization-wide strategy for Lean implementation in alignment with the top leadership,
- Ensuring Lean is an integral part of the larger improvement roadmap of the organization,
- Assisting value stream and functional leaders to unfurl opportunities for improvement,

[3] Taken from Debashis Sarkar's book *Lean for Service Organizations and Offices: A Holistic Approach for Achieving Operational Excellence* (ASQ Press, USA, 2008).

- Providing thought leadership on matters pertaining to Lean and other improvement methods,
- Ensuring that the Lean practice effectively develops, manages and exploits knowledge within the organization and that value streams/functions are able to access this knowledge with ease,
- Helping to create capabilities for Lean implementation within the various functions and value streams,
- Keeping tabs on emerging trends in the domain of improvements and Lean process excellence,
- Interacting with cutting-edge technology experts and leveraging these resources for improvements,
- Providing assurance to the Chief Executive and respective functional leaders on the health of the processes and overall Lean management system,
- Facilitating both internal as well as external benchmarking,
- Housing experts on multiple improvement approaches such as Lean, Six Sigma, Lean Sigma, Lean Process Management,
- Advancing the reputation of the organization by showcasing the work done on Lean and improvements.

Remember, irrespective of the type of organization, a Lean office is imperative for the transformation.

Key Takeaways

- Failing to install a Lean office in a company will quickly flatten the benefits reaped through Lean projects.
- The Lean office should report to the top management of the company and should be headed by the Chief Improvement Officer or Lean Leader.
- The Lean office should guide the CEO and other members of the top management on improvements and on the steps the organization should take to be more competitive and agile.
- The Lean office is a strategic think-tank and should house some of the best resources of the company.

Lesson 31

THE ROLE OF THE LEAN OFFICE SHOULD CHANGE OVER TIME

We discussed installing a Lean office in Lesson 30. However, the role and composition of this corporate team should change as implementation matures in the company. After the first few years of deployment, it would not be wise to expect the Lean office to function in the same way as it did in the early years of the Lean journey.

In the first few years of Lean implementation, the focus of the central Lean office should be on awareness creation, getting organizational engagement and taking ownership for initiating improvements in various parts of the organization. The focus should also be on building capabilities across the length and breadth of the firm and creating a solid block of knowledge and experience relevant to the company. The major focus of the Lean office should be to get the right engagement, hold hands and demonstrate how to carry out improvements. Remember, in this phase the Lean office is one central team that takes substantial ownership for deployment by facilitating Lean adoption amongst the business units/value streams.

However, as time passes, the complexion of the team should change. The size of the Lean office should reduce by half. The implementation of Lean should shift to the respective value streams and business groups as business units and value-stream owners take ownership for Lean implementation and leverage it for reaping business results. Once this happens, the Lean office is needed only when specific technical inputs are required.

In this phase, the Lean office focuses on capability building, best-practice sharing and tracking ongoing performance. The Lean mavens who were earlier with the Lean office gradually move into business units and act as resources there. In this phase the Lean office is also available for specific facilitation such as project selection. As the Lean journey matures, the Lean office gets decentralized and each business group and value stream installs their own small Lean offices.

Remember, when Lean projects are carried out across an enterprise, integrating the firm-wide gains can often be difficult, especially in large companies. This is because of lack of knowledge among Lean office teams of the different value streams and the diverse customers they cater to. To have decentralized Lean offices in the early days of implementation is not a good idea though. This will not work, as business and functional heads may not treat Lean foundation building as their goal when they are busy achieving business targets.

Figure 3.13 summarizes the changing roles of the Lean office.

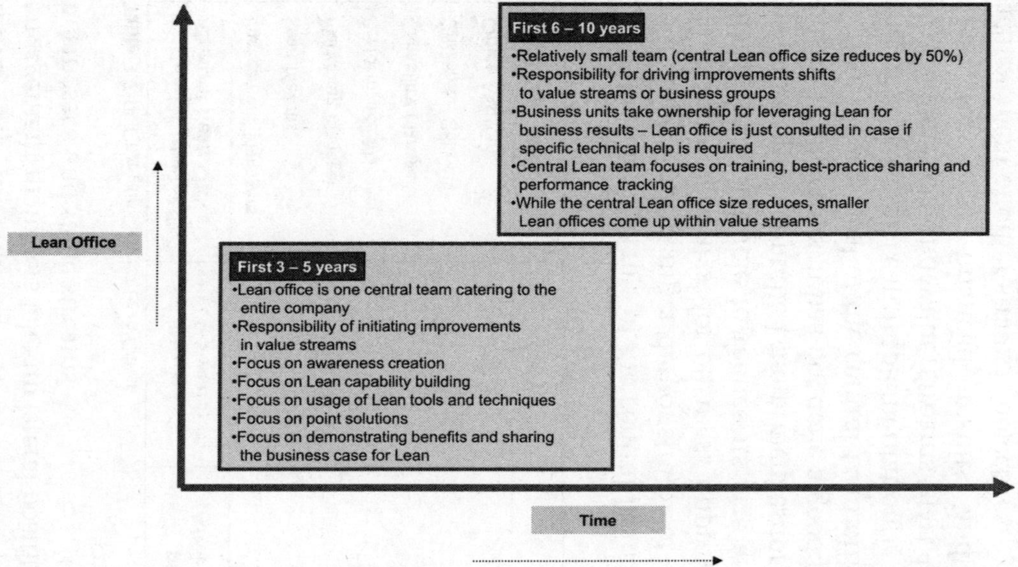

Fig 3.13: The Changing Complexion of the Lean Office

Table 3.7 summarizes the changes within the central Lean office of a global company. The Lean mavens move into the various value streams while the engagement managers take up lateral positions within businesses and value streams.

Table 3.7: A Changing Central Lean Office

Composition of Central Lean Office	Phase 1 (3–5 years)	Phase 2 (After 3–5 years)
Engagement Managers	6	1
Lean Mavens	12	2
Marketing Manager	1	—
Performance Manager	1	1
Capability Manager	1	1
Customer Cells	3	3
Office Assistant	1	1
Total	**25**	**9**

Remember, the role of the central Lean office has to change from being a demonstrator of Lean-as-a-value-add to a catalyst for business improvement. If this team is not able to reduce its size and ensure business units adopt the Lean principles for achieving business objectives, it has not done a good job.

The biggest goal of the central Lean office during the first phase of Lean implementation is to ensure that businesses and value streams start leveraging Lean for their financial results and for the achievement of other strategic objectives.

Key Takeaways
■ The role of the Lean office should change over a period of time. ■ The Lean office should continually upgrade skills which can take the organization to greater heights. ■ If the size of Lean office increases over a period of time (say after five years), it could be an indication that there is lack of foresight on the management's part about what Lean can do to improve business. ■ If you see that Lean is not delivering additional benefits over a period of time, it could indicate the need to decentralize the Lean offices within the business units/ functions/value streams of the organization.

Lesson 32

EMBED A3 THINKING

A3 thinking is the practice of using a single sheet of paper for solving problems, sharing proposals and strategic planning. Since A3-sized paper (11 × 17 inches) is used for this purpose, it is called A3 thinking. Developed in the Toyota stable, the concept can be used in any type of industry and forces teams to share their story in a short and standardized manner.

The A3 sheet can be used for problem solving, strategic planning, proposal writing and status reporting. The focus in this lesson is on problem solving.

The structure of the A3 sheet is such that it provides a brilliant approach to PDCA management. PDCA or Plan-Do-Check-Act is Deming's approach to problem solving and has been discussed in detail in Lesson 44, but it is summarized in Table 3.8.

Table 3.8: PDCA and Problem Solving Steps

PDCA	Steps
Plan	Background, Current State, Goal, Root Cause Analysis
Do	Countermeasures
Check	Confirmation of Results
Act	Follow-up Actions

The A3 report actually creates a storyline of the way the problem has been resolved. Figure 3.14 on the next page shows the template for problem solving with numbered steps. The seven steps in the A3 template follow a PDCA approach. As you can see, steps 1–4 comprise fifty per cent of the A3 sheet. This shows the importance of planning in problem solving. An important lesson here is that we need to spend a lot of time understanding the current state before getting into implementation. It also acts as a visual tool wherein the problem's details are scripted and members get involved in giving inputs to solve it.

Use a pencil to write the details so that things can be written and changed based on inputs received from teams. The steps can be changed by the companies based on their context, but the general approach to be followed is the same. The focus should be to make the problem visual so that it can be understood easily.

Name of the Company: __________, Business Unit: ________,
Workplace: ________, Project Name: ________, Project Id: ________
Team Leader: ________, Team Members: __________

1. Background	5. Countermeasures
2. Current State	6. Confirmation of Results
3. Goal	7. Follow-up Actions and Sustainability Imperatives
4. Root Cause Analysis	

Fig 3.14: Template for A3 Problem Solving

Now the question arises, how do you implement A3 thinking in your company? Here are a few things that you can do to accomplish this:

- Take a strategic call to adopt A3 sheets,
- Train all employees on A3 problem solving,
- Put a ban on long presentations and make A3 sheets the only way for problem solution,
- Managers and leaders need to be adept in interpreting the finer nuances of A3 problem solving.

The A3 sheet can also be used for strategic planning (Figure 3.15) and proposals (Figure 3.16) as shown on the next two pages.

Just imagine what A3 thinking can do:

- Eliminate long problem-solving presentations,
- Reduce the time spent in presentations
- Eliminate long project review meetings as stand-in reviews would happen where the action happens,
- Facilitate better and fewer meetings,
- Force teams to understand the problem statement adequately before getting into solutions,
- Bring visibility to the problem solving process,
- Embed simplicity,
- Facilitate systematic thinking among employees,
- Help seniors to mentor team members as any change in process would require the buy in of the bosses which is a great mentoring opportunity,
- Avoid creating communication gaps between teams as the problem-solving approach is before them and they know the flow,
- Prevent teams from taking short-cuts,

1. Last Year's Performance	5. Detailed Action Plan
2. Reflection of Last Year's Performance	**6. Critical Success Factors**
3. Current Year's Objectives	**7. Before and After Metrics**
4. Justification for this year's focus area	**8. Issues pending:**

Fig 3.15: A3 Template for Strategic Planning

Name of the Company: ________, Business Unit: ________,
Workplace: ________, Project Name: ________, Project Id: ________
Team Leader: ________, Team Members: ____________________

1. Background

2. Current State

3. Proposal Details

4. Dissection and Analysis

5. Plan Highlights

6. RACI* and Time Lines

* Responsible, Accountable, Consulted and Informed

Fig 3.16: A3 Template for Proposal Writing

- Act as a knowledge repository,
- Compel a standardized approach to problem solving using PDCA cycle,
- Foster better team work and collaboration among team members.

To know more about A3 thinking, I would recommend you go through the research work of Durward K. Sobek at the University of Montana and John Shook at Lean Enterprises.

Key Takeaways
■ A3 thinking is the practice of using a single sheet of paper for problem solving. ■ A3 thinking is a brilliant mechanism to build logical and systematic thinking in a company. ■ A3 thinking is more than a tool, it is a philosophy. ■ A3 thinking has multiple applications such as problem solving, strategic planning, proposal writing etc.

Lesson 33

Follow A Holistic Approach to Visual Management System

Making workplaces visual is an integral part of Lean deployment. However, let me tell you that workplaces will not be visually managed just by wishing it. Teams will not be able to adopt and practice visual tools for performance excellence merely by being aware of visual management. What leaders need to know is that we need a holistic approach to installing and institutionalizing a visual management system. For this, an approach has to be put together by the Lean maven and kept in mind as the Lean journey progresses. Together with this, leaders have to create an environment wherein teams are encouraged to come up with various ideas for visual tools that can be used in managing workplace performance.

These tools will change as the journey of Lean matures and different interventions come to play. The worst thing is when someone reads about a set of tools in a book and simply implements them indiscriminately in the workplace. The type of techniques used should be driven by the type of Lean intervention underway. You will see that the visual management tools change, get replaced and also improve over a period of time. The tools have to be relevant to the context. All the visual techniques in a workplace have to work in tandem to meet the larger organizational objectives.

Figure 3.17 shows an approach which can be kept in mind while instilling visual management in an organization. You need to remember that this approach has a service industry bias, but a similar one could be devised for a manufacturing company also.

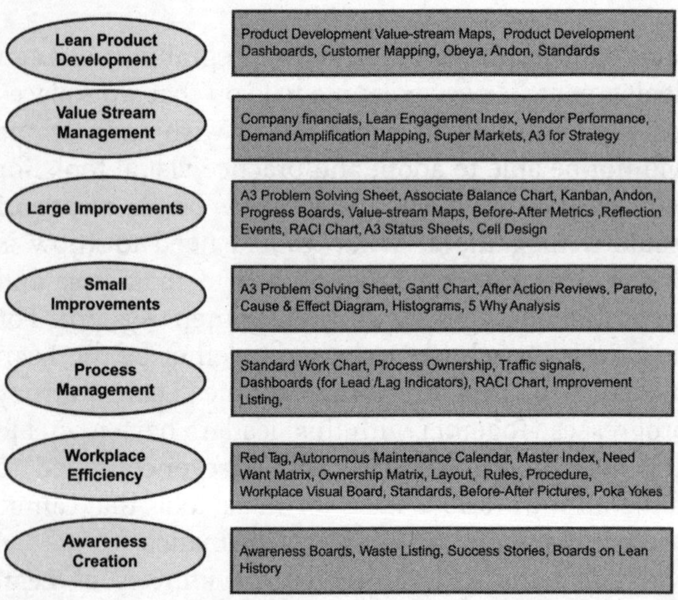

Fig 3.17: Approach for Visual Management

It may be noted that the visual tools showed in Figure 3.17 are not comprehensive. The objective here is to give a glimpse into some of the relevant tools at relevant points of the Lean transformation based on the initiative underway. Also, the various initiatives shown in Figure 3.17 may not be sequential as depicted. Organizations can have these interventions in a different sequence.

As the organization migrates up the chart or matures in its Lean journey, some of the foundational visual tools may remain while others may be replaced with newer ones. For example, in the early days of Lean implementation, when awareness creation is the objective, we could inundate the workplace with posters on Lean basics and wastes. However, once a process management system is built, many of the posters on Lean basics/wastes could be replaced with standard work sheets, metrics, dashboards etc.

It should be kept in mind that visual management tools have two broad purposes. They are used for information sharing and also for managing performance. It is critical that a workplace should have a balance of both the types. On average, 40–45 per cent should be information sharing and the rest should be for management and improvement of performance.

Visual techniques need not necessarily be only visual but could be enmeshed with audio signals, like a siren.

You also need to keep in mind that the types of visual management used during a project would be quite different from the ones that are used for day-to-day management of performance. The former would typically be like a war-room while the latter will be in the work place where the day-to-day actions happen.

I would recommend appointing a person who can manage visual management in a workplace. This is a part-time role but this individual keeps leaders informed on the health of the visual system. Of course, s/he is only a provider of tools and techniques; the work has to be done by the teams.

In fields such as financial services, usage of information technology could be essential, especially when processes happen in electronic space and cut through geographies and functions. Remember, visual management displays can never hide in your respective computers. Even if they are digital, they have to be visible to all impacted in a workplace.

Key Takeaways
■ Visual tools should be used for sharing information and also for managing performance. ■ Keep a holistic strategy for building an effective visual management system. ■ Doing ad hoc visual management can never help in managing workplace performance. ■ The type of visual management tools used will change as the Lean journey matures. ■ Make one person responsible for managing the visual management tools in a workplace.

Lesson 34

Institutionalize the Process of Reflection

As a part of Lean thinking, embed a culture of 'reflection' in your company. After every project or assignment gets completed, make your teams ponder on what could have been done better. Install a process to find out what went well and what did not.

The Japanese call this process *Hansei* which literally means self-reflection. It is an integral part of Japanese culture wherein an individual acknowledges his or her mistake and commits to carrying out the necessary improvement. The Japanese society constantly pushes its politicians to carry out Hansei and mend their corrupt ways. In Toyota, teams conduct Hansei events on a regular basis, during Lean breakthroughs etc. The outcome of the Hansei event is looped back to improve products or processes. Taichi Ohno used the Check phase in the PDCA cycle as Hansei. As you begin Lean implementation, create a learning organization by practicing Hansei on a regular basis.

Beyond Japan, the US army has a brilliant process of reflection which they call After Action Reviews (AAR). They are among a very few organizations in the world to have institutionalized this process. The AAR is an assessment discussion to improve the effectiveness of teams. The objective of AAR is to identify what was supposed to happen, what actually happened, why it happened, and how to sustain strengths and improve on weaknesses.

So, how does one go about installing a good reflection process? Figure 3.18 shows the process which can be followed:

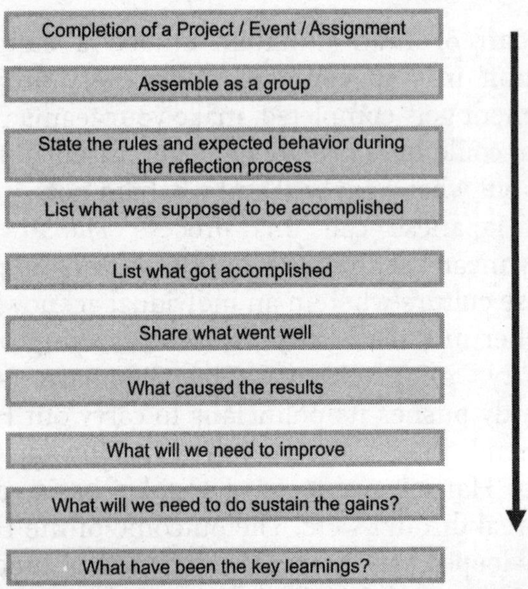

Fig 3.18: Process for Reflection

Reflection has to be both an intellectual and emotional exercise. It helps the team members to dissect the entire project/assignment in a non-threatening manner. When you start the reflection process in your company, it will take time for members to open up. Leaders have to be patient, and should create an environment for the members to open up. All individuals in the company should undergo training on how to facilitate a process of reflection.

Table 3.9 summarizes the dos and don'ts of a reflection process which you should always remember.

Table 3.9: Do's and Don'ts of a Reflection Process

- Never criticize a person.
- Capture the war stories and lessons learnt.
- Probe why certain actions were taken.
- Discuss in sufficient detail so that everyone understands.
- Make juniors lead the discussion.
- Do not lecture and sermonize.
- The reflection process can happen before, during and after the event.
- Can be used in any process/context wherein there is repetitive work.
- Should bring out the training needs of individual team members.
- Use open-ended questions.
- Involve all participants in the discussion.
- Focus on both individual and team performance.
- Have the reflection as soon as the project gets over.
- Make sure everyone is on board before completing the reflection event.

Even if the project has been successful, do carry out the reflection process. There will always be learnings, opportunities for improvement and sustainability challenges to discuss. It is a brilliant engine to make tacit knowledge explicit.

Key Takeaways
■ Reflection is one of the most under-used tools for learning and improvement. ■ Reflection is a process which helps to improve the effectiveness of not just the individuals but also the team. It also creates leaders for organizational transformation. ■ Leaders at all levels should practice reflection. ■ Reflection should be both an intellectual and emotional exercise.

Lesson 35

Institutionalize LIP-SIP Engine for Improvements

The implementation of Lean requires that an engine be created which allows improvement projects of all complexions to be performed. I have observed organizations embarking on a Lean journey doing a few improvement projects and thinking that the right thing is being done. Another approach which organizations often take is to just focus on high-impact projects. For them the focus of the Lean transformation is just to worry about projects which have a large impact on costs and revenues. While there is nothing wrong with such projects, the approach is incomplete. What is recommended here is that we follow the LIP-SIP construct of improvements.

So, what is the LIP-SIP construct of improvements?

It is an approach to improvements wherein Large Improvement Projects (LIP) are backed with a large number of Small Improvement Projects (SIP), as shown in Figure 3.19.

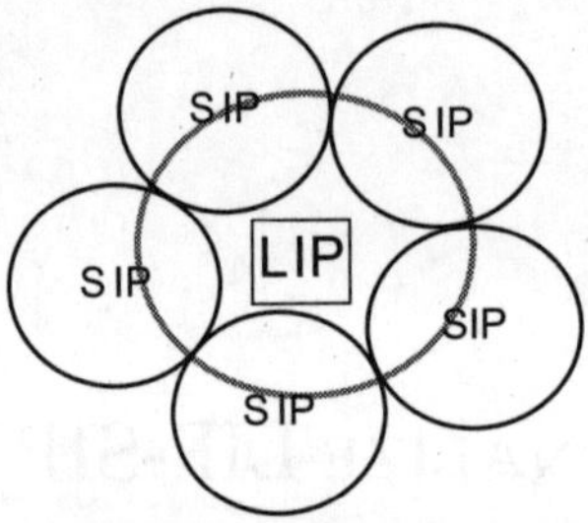

Fig 3.19: LIP–SIP Construct of Improvements

So, what are Large Improvement Projects (LIP) and Small Improvement Projects (SIP)?

Large Improvement Projects (LIP):
These are large cross-functional projects taken up on key processes to deliver benefits to the bottom line. These projects take up to three to four months to complete and are driven by senior leaders. They require the participation of teams representing all stakeholders such as process, product, policy, risk, information technology and so on. These projects have an objective to bring about a sea change in the way processes are currently performed in the company. They are either sponsored by the top management or are led by middle management.

Small Improvement Projects (SIP):
These are short duration projects to be completed within two to three weeks, which are taken up by associates working on the shop floor using elementary quality improvement tools. The target of these projects is to address local issues, which are not on the radar of

the leaders driving large projects. These projects have the major objective of garnering employee involvement in improvements and building a culture of improvements *by the employees, for the employees, of the employees.* Local leaders who could be a part of junior management team sponsor these projects. Table 3.10 gives examples of projects in both these categories.

Table 3.10: Examples of Large and Small Improvement Projects

	Type of Project	Sponsor	Example
1.	Large Improvement Project	Top Management	Improving the way mortgage business is done by moving from a brick and mortar model to leveraging multiple channels
2.	Large Improvement Project	Middle Management	Reduction of end to end disbursement lead times of mortgage processing
3.	Small Improvement Project	Junior Management	Improving the productivity of processing associates in a credit shop

Both large and small improvement projects are endowed with some inherent strengths which complement each other and are a must for solid improvement in the company. Large projects are done on critical business processes of the organization, while small projects target local workplace issues and small work processes and procedures. The beauty of small projects is that they do not require large investments and help in building a solid foundation of quality by rooting a culture of continual improvement. Employees take them up voluntarily to address specific issues impacting their workplace for their own benefit. When organizations just focus on large projects, improvements are centred on a set of experts who arrive, perform and carry out improvements.

In the eyes of the shop floor individuals, large project implementation is about people like Lean Mavens swooping into their workplace like extra-terrestrials, facilitating a set of solutions and then flying out. To them it is adopting something triggered by someone else, which they have to internalize. Further, it could appear that an improvement has been enforced upon them. Remember, improvements that are pushed by someone else and have been adopted in a half-hearted manner cannot be sustained and gradually deteriorate. Even if there is a high degree of acceptance for such solutions, the chances of any system degrading over a period of time is imminent. Given this context, it is imperative that all large projects are backed with a large number of small projects, which are led and taken up for implementation by the associates working in the processes on the shop floor. This implies that one large project should be associated or followed by a large number of small projects

For the larger organization, this would mean a Deming's Wheel of improvement (Figure 3.20) functioning in the company embedded with Large and Small Improvement Projects.

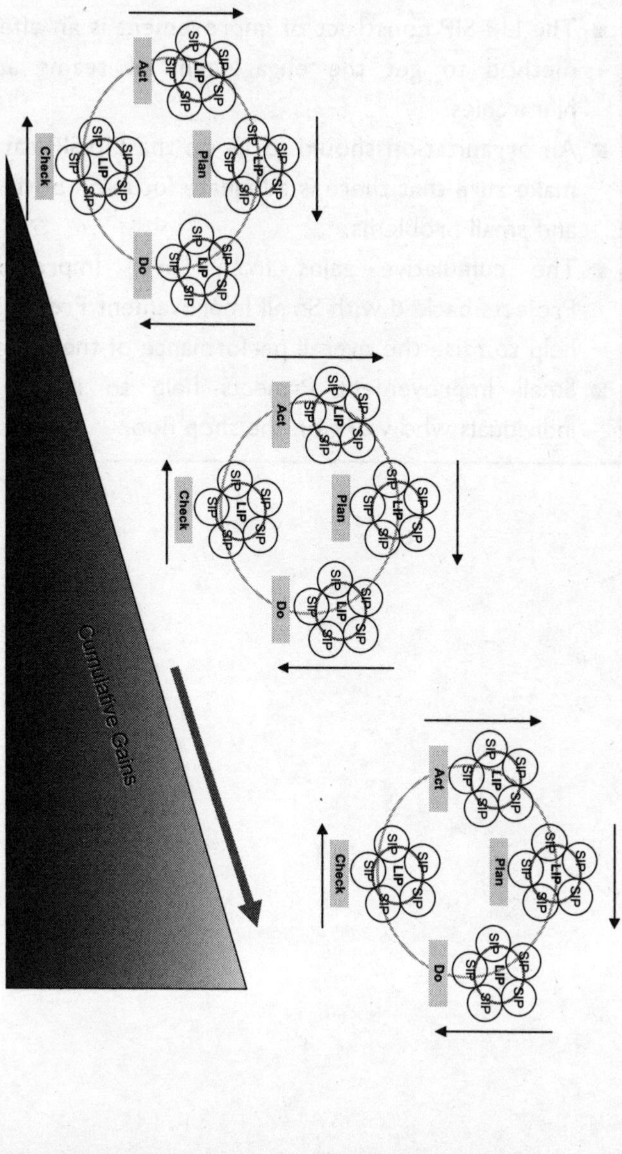

Fig 3.20: Small and Large Improvement Projects in Deming's Wheel

Key Takeaways

- The LIP-SIP construct of improvement is an effective method to get the engagement of teams across hierarchies.
- An organization should focus on the LIP:SIP ratio to make sure that there is adequate focus on both large and small problems.
- The cumulative gains from Large Improvement Projects backed with Small Improvement Projects will help to raise the overall performance of the company.
- Small Improvement Projects help to involve the individuals who work on the shop floor.

Section 4

Problem-Solving

Problem-Solving

Problem Solving is an integral part of Lean management. All leaders need to imbibe problem solving skills and understand the context where the problem has occurred to solve it, along with the help of the teams working there. Thought leaders of Lean management such as James Womack and Jeffery Liker have written extensively on the problem-solving approach followed at Toyota. The following are key facets distilled from their research which need to be kept in mind while building a problem-solving culture:

- **Rigour**: Teams need rigour. Short cuts do not really yield the desired results.
- **Engagement**: Teams need to be positively involved in coming up with solutions.
- **Context**: The problems need to be solved at the place where they have occurred.
- **Leadership**: Leaders mentor and challenge teams to come up with the best solutions.
- **Experimentation**: Problems get solved by proper experimentation. Failures lead to knowledge which can be used in the future.
- **Tools**: Using the right set of tools is essential to get the desired results.
- **Structure**: Follow a uniform approach for solving problems across the organization.
- **Knowledge**: As you solve problems, you should create knowledge for future use.

Lesson 36

Ohno's Wastes are Applicable to Service Organizations

Many Lean practitioners tell me that the eight wastes of Lean as advocated by Taichi Ohno are not applicable in service companies. This is not true. Kudos to the work done by Mr. Ohno: these wastes are applicable across businesses in all contexts and situations. Let me list the eight wastes with specific examples from service businesses (Table 4.1 on the next page) to demonstrate that the works created in manufacturing are also applicable to services.

The key here is to identify the above unseen wastes when they occur. This is not easy especially because individuals bound to a workplace tend to ignore what's happening there. I call it the Ostrich Syndrome. Most organizations over a period of time become a victim of the Ostrich Syndrome. The larger the organization, the bigger the likelihood of this problem.

Table 4.1: Eight Wastes of Lean (with examples)

S No.	Type of Waste (Symptom)	What does it mean	Examples
1.	Waste of Over-production	Processing more or sooner than required	• Purchasing items before they are needed • Processing paperwork before the next person is ready for it • Franked loan agreements lying unutilized • Promotional materials printed more than required
2.	Waste of Motion	Unnecessary movement of individuals for successfully completing a job in a process	• Multiple visits by sales people to get the right documents from the customers • Scattered departments in an organization • Zigzag movement of documents during the processing of an application form in a process shop • Walking to/from copier, central filing, fax machine while executing a process
3.	Waste of Inventory	Refers to items/ supplies in the process which are more than single piece, flow or movement of items. In service businesses single piece may not be possible, so it is about supplies/ items being more than required	• Documents lying in a workplace because they have not been lifted by courier on time • Piles of loan files lying in branches/credit shops • More stationery or IT equipment in a workplace than is required • Documents/records lying around beyond their retention period
4.	Waste of Transportation	Refers to movement of materials, more than required.	• Excessive email attachments • Multiple hand-offs • Multiple approvals • Files moving from one branch to another

Table 4.1: Eight Wastes of Lean (with examples)

S No.	Type of Waste (Symptom)	What does it mean	Examples
5.	Waste of Waiting	Refers to individuals and items being idle between operations	• Customers waiting in a bank branch/grocery store • Files and documents waiting for signatures/ approval • Associates waiting for earlier processes to finish • New employees waiting for infrastructure • Customer waiting in phone banking/call centre queue
6.	Waste of Under-Utilized people	Refers to employees in a process not being utilized to the fullest	• Employee talent not being leveraged • Individual put on the wrong job • Incorrect selection of a candidate for a job
7.	Waste of Defects	Refers to waste that occurs due to errors and not getting the processing right the first time	• Error in filling a cell-phone application form • Incorrect name being placed on a cheque book
8.	Waste of Over-processing	Refers to efforts in a process, which add no value to the customer	• Sending a document by overnight courier service when an ordinary courier service would suffice • Redundant steps in a process • Multiple inspections in a process • Lack of operator training • Undefined or unclear customer requirements

Ostrich syndrome sets in further when the company is growing at a fast rate and leaders find it futile to spend time on uncovering wastes. The only way to reduce and arrest this problem is awareness among employees and coaching them to see the wastes in their respective workplaces. This is a major change exercise in an organization's Lean transformation as it requires employees to do so voluntarily.

Key Takeaways
■ Making employees appreciate the various types of wastes is the first step in Lean improvement. ■ Find out how many people in your workplace are victims of the Ostrich Syndrome. ■ From president to janitor, everyone in the organization should know how to identify the wastes. ■ Beyond a point it does not matter which of the eight wastes a particular instance of waste is. What is required is to identify that the waste is occuring. Do not squander time in branding them. ■ Often wastes have a knock-on effect. One waste leads to the other.

Lesson 37

Inventory in a Services Context can be Quite Esoteric

One of the key objectives of Lean is inventory reduction. This can be quite a challenge in a service context. In a manufacturing company, inventory is tangible and includes things such as raw materials, semi-finished goods, rejects etc. These are visible, so it is clear that reducing inventory will uncover waste. Having learnt to see waste, attacking it becomes easier. However, in a service context this can be quite difficult. Inventory may not always be tangible and visible, so working on the waste reduction can be quite a challenge.

To understand what an inventory in a process is, you need to think about the **use** and **consume** principles of processes. In every process, there are things which get used and there are items which get consumed.

Those items which transform and change their shape, form and state as a part of the process are **consumed**. Let us take an example from the automobile world. Items that get consumed while manufacturing a car include things such as steel or plastic which are processed to produce a car. The form and shape of the raw material changes and transforms into the final product. In a services context, the items which get **consumed** may not have a physical transformation, but their state may change. For example, in a mortgage finance business, the status of the form changes from an unapproved state to an approved state.

In contrast, **used** items are those which are required during processing but do not transform by the end of the process. In the case of a car manufacturer, such items could be people, machines etc. In mortgage processing, the typical items which get **used** include people, computers, infrastructure and so on.

Making all employees understand and appreciate the inventories in service processes is the first step towards waste optimization. The typical inventory in the service industry could be the following:

- Emails,
- Files,
- Documents,
- Data,
- Information,
- Electronic reports and documents.

So, when you have to identify inventory in service processes, question and see if it is being consumed. If the answer is in the affirmative, it is a target for inventory reduction. In Lesson 49 we will look at Little's Law which comes very handy while working on inventory reduction.

Just remember, humans who are involved in the processes can never be treated as inventory. These are those people who run the process. So, never treat customers as inventory. However, there are some exceptions. While working on leaning an HR process such as recruitment, humans are to be treated as inventory. Also, in customer-facing entities such as retail branches, stores, supermarkets, when you are working towards reducing wait times, customers will be treated as inventory

Key Takeaways
■ Identifying what is inventory in a service process is quite critical. ■ Service processes can have inventories of various types such as paper, documents, e-mails, data etc. ■ Making teams appreciate unseen inventories especially in virtual or electronic space can be quite challenging. ■ Without fundamental changes in the process, inventory reduction will only provide temporary results and the process can slide back to a sea of growing inventory.

FROM THE TRENCHES: Excess cash holding in bank branches calls for a Lean intervention

In bank branches holding more cash than required impacts the profitability of the branches. This is because cash available but not deployed is a lost revenue opportunity for the bank. Branches with large volumes of cash, apart from being a big risk, affect the profitability of the bank, as cash kept in the safe does not generate interest.

Under my guidance a team took up a project to reduce the average-cash-holding of branches in a large financial service conglomerate. The principles of Lean were used to solve this problem. As part of the roll out the following principles were used:

- Waste Identification,
- Cycle Time study,
- Small Batch Size,
- Standard Work procedures,
- Flow,
- Pull.

As a part of the project execution, the following types of wastes shown in Table 4.2, on the facing page, were identified.

Lean principles can be applied in almost all sections of the bank, as can be seen via Figure 4.1 on the facing page, which shows how pull was created in the process.

The intervention saw around 40 per cent reduction in cash-holding.

(*Continued*)

Table 4.2: Wastes Observed in Cash Projects

What was observed	Type of waste
Cash bundling not handled by tellers	Waste of Under-utilized people
Excess cash indented	Waste of Overproduction
Cash vehicle movement	Waste of Transportation
Cash waiting to be bundled	Waste of Waiting
Left over processed cash involves re-binding and packaging for offload	Waste of Over-processing
Un-processed cash lying in vault	Waste of Inventory

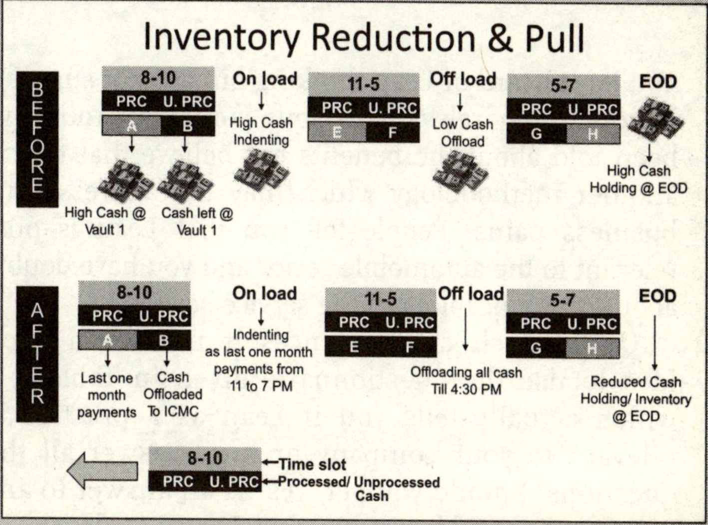

Fig 4.1: Pull in a Cash Management Process in a Retail Branch

Lesson 38

Administer the Opportunity Questionnaire to Judge Lean Applicability

You have heard of Lean thinking but are not sure if it is something relevant to your company. You have been told about the benefits but believe that this is another methodology which may not address your business pains. People tell you that Lean is only relevant to the automobile sector and you have doubts about its applicability in the service sector.

Under such circumstances it may be a good idea to use the questionnaire given in Table 4.3, which actually tells you if Lean as a practice is relevant to your company or not. Answer all the questions. Should you get 'yes' as an answer to any of them, it would indicate that Lean is relevant to your business.

Table 4.3 Deb's Lean Opportunity Questionnaire

S No	Questions	Yes/No
1	Are there chronic issues about which customers continually complain?	
2	Is the number of employees increasing in proportion to the increase in sales volume?	
3	Are there core processes which do not have ownership?	
4	Do you see the capabilities of team members not being used to the fullest?	
5	Do you see a large number of MIS reports being generated which no-one looks at?	
6	Do you see teams spending a lot of time fire-fighting?	
7	Do you see a lot of silo issues and teams not talking among themselves?	
8	Are there follow-up teams whose job is to coordinate and get things done among departments?	
9	Are error/defect levels high in processes?	
10	Are there critical issues which do not have ownership because of which they are not getting attention?	
11	Do processes get automated whenever there are bottlenecks and hurdles?	
12	Are there a large number of auditors and inspectors to ensure no defects occur in the process?	
13	Do teams get instituted to spend time on process work-rounds?	
14	Are there teams to manage and correct customer problems?	
15	Is a lot of the time spent on urgent issues, customer complaints and process corrections?	

Table 4.3 Deb's Lean Opportunity Questionnaire (*continued*)

S No	Questions	Yes/No
16	Are there teams dedicated for exception management?	
17	Are there units within the business which do not have well-defined processes?	
18	Are there issues pertaining to consistency of delivery?	
19	Are there issues of managing scale and growing volumes?	
20	Are there processes or business operations which have become complex over a period of time?	
21	Are there products/brands added over a period of time which are not profitable today?	
22	Are there non-profitable customers who cannot be weeded out?	
23	Are the efficiency ratios of your business going up? (* For example, efficiency in banking measured by cost/income ratios)	
24	Are you finding it difficult to manage a large number of products or service variants?	
25	Is there a proliferation of channels and products which you are finding difficult to manage?	
26	Is there a dire need to create capacity within your business to manage future needs?	
27	Is your business finding it difficult to survive the cost and competitive pressures of the marketplace?	
28	Is there a need to simplify your business processes and structures?	
29	Is there a need felt for having more flexible business processes and systems?	

While the questionnaire is not a solution to your problems it will definitely give you an idea if Lean is the right thing for your business or not. However, it should be noted that such questionnaires are very directional, and detailed assessment should be done before getting into a Lean engagement.

Key Takeaways
■ Lean is not a panacea for all business maladies but can help provide solutions to a large number of business problems. ■ Even the most agile and efficient business would always have the opportunity for Lean application. ■ Lean not only makes a business efficient but also effective. ■ Whenever in doubt, use the questionnaire to see if Lean is relevant for your business or not.

Lesson 39

Make Customers Serve Themselves

One of the objectives of Lean intervention should be to create an environment wherein customers can serve themselves. Do not be amazed at what I am telling you. Some people believe that by making customers serve themselves, you will be alienating them. This is not true. This is an old shibboleth that one cannot cling to in today's fast-paced world of customer service. There are ample examples today to prove that self-service is something which customers readily accept and find very convenient.

So, what are the benefits of self-service? The following is a list of key benefits that an organization can reap from customer service:

- Self-service provides better customer convenience,
- Customers can transact with the organization at their own wish, at their desired time from a

desired context (especially in case of web-based transactions),

- Opportunities for service failures go down as there is reduction in human intervention—like it or not, humans are a major cause of process failures,
- Eliminates wastes in process,
- Drives cost efficiency,
- Gives the customer a sense of control,
- No need to wait to speak to an executive from the customer perspective,
- Helps to reduce the customer's interaction time with the organization.

However, organizations need to know that whatever self-service they provide has to be engaging and value-adding. If the customers do not see the self-service options to be value-adding, the entire endeavour is going to be a waste.

The following are some of the examples of self-service options which organizations have provided to customers:

- ATM for cash withdrawal from a bank,
- Mobile phones for utility payments,
- Kiosks for airline check-in,
- Web check-in from home,
- Interactive Voice Response (IVR) in a call center.

Self-service strategies can be driven with the objective of either cost efficiency or customer convenience. My recommendation is that a Lean implementation should focus on both of them. However, we need to remember the following while creating a mechanism for self-service for the customers:

- Do not make self-service an objective of the Lean process improvement. It should emerge as one of the solutions.
- Before providing self-service solutions, complete a thorough value-added/non-value-added analysis.
- A customer self-service solution should not appear as something which has been pushed by the company but something needed by the customer.
- Pinpoint the customer-segment which is being targeted by the self-service solution.
- Focus on providing the right customer experience.
- The self-service experience has to be the same as or better than other available channels.
- Make sure that the customer is able to navigate the self-service option easily.
- Buttress the self-service product with a marketing and customer communication blitzkrieg if need be.
- Constantly listen to the customer—Be ready to continually change/improve the self-service channel based on customer requirements.
- Provide training to customers so that they get comfortable using the self-service channel (Incentivize customer-service agents to do it, if needed.)
- Incentivize customers to adopt the self-service channel.
- Leverage superior technology wherever required to provide better customer convenience.

From my experience I have seen that self-service is a brilliant solution when you have a large number of customers to take care of (as in banks, airlines, travel agencies etc). The self-service channel should solve some of the problems which the customer currently faces, or else one may find it difficult to create an impact. But remember, if ease and convenience are impacted, customers may return to the earlier channel. Last but not the least; do not push the self-service channel. Give them a choice and engage them to adopt it for their personal betterment.

Key Takeaways
■ A Lean process improvement should not be targeted to create a self-service channel; rather self-service should be one of the solutions emerging from team deliberations. ■ A self-service channel should be easy to navigate for the customer.

Lesson 40

Do not Forget Waste in Functional Cervices

While leaning your organization, one of the things that you should look for within each of the functions/ departments/roles is waste. It has been observed that over a period of time, redundancies set into these areas which need to be eliminated. These can be in the following form:

- **Efforts not valued:** Functions and departments wasting time on activities which are not relevant.
- **Overlapping of roles:** Two or more roles doing the same activities.
- **Duplication of functions/departments:** Similar functions/departments in other parts of the organization.

So, how does one go about leaning an organizational function/structure while addressing the above issues?

How to Tackle Efforts that do not add Value

Step 1: Departmental Overview Listing

List all the vital details of a specific department/ function. You can use the template shown in Table 4.4

Table 4.4 Functional Overview Listing

What is the mission of the department/function?
What are the key deliverables of the department/function?
How does the department/function contribute to the larger organizational objective?
What are the key activities of this role?
Who are the customers* of the department/function?

* Customers could also be internal customers or other functions/departments within the company.

Step 2: Value Contribution of Listed Activities in a Function

The value contribution of the activities listed in the earlier step needs to be ascertained with respect to the department/function. This is explained visually in Figure 4.2 on the next page.

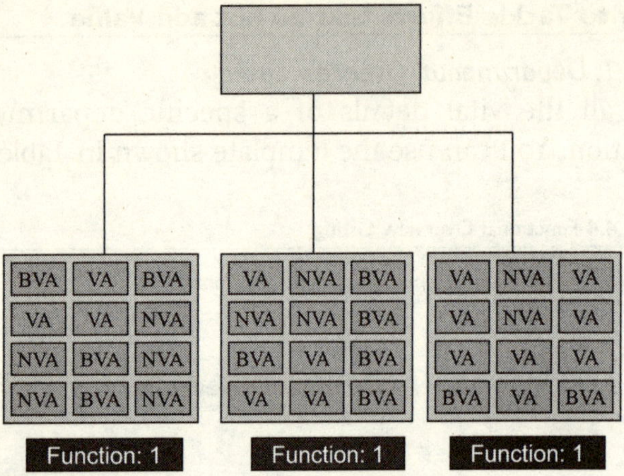

Fig 4.2: Value-Added (VA), Non-Value-Added (NVA), Business-Value-Added (BVA) Activity in a Function

- **Value Added Activity:**

For an activity to be a value-added one from a department/function's perspective, we should look at it through a Lean lens and answer the questions posed in Table 4.5 below.

You should get affirmative answers to all the questions in the table if the activity does provide a value-addition. Negative answers mean that the activity is Non-Value-Added.

Table 4.5 Questions for Value-Added Activity

S No	Questions	Yes/No
1	Is the activity being done for the customer?	
2	Does the activity contribute towards achieving the organizational objectives?	
3	Is this being done for something which is "right-first-time"?	

- **Business-Value-Added Activity:**

Beyond these activities there could also be actions which do not contribute towards the meeting of organizational objectives. In such a case the questions listed in Table 4.6 below need to be answered.

For an activity to be business-value-added, you should get affirmative answers to all the questions in the Table. Negative answers mean that the activity is Non-Value Added.

Table 4.6 Questions for Business-Value-Added Activity

S No	Questions	Yes/No
1	Is the activity being done for the customer?	
2	Is the activity required for control or to meet statutory/regulatory/environmental stipulations?	

All other activities done in the department are non-value-added. These activities should be eliminated.

Remember, these activities within functions should not be mixed with the tasks that get scrutinized while looking for wastes in processes.

Tackling Role Duplication

Step 1: List all the activities done in a department/function

Brainstorm all the activities done in a department comprehensively. The template given in Table 4.4 on the next page lists some of the key activities done by the department. Ensure that each of the activities has a unique nomenclature and number. This will help in unique identification and treating the data easily.

Table 4.7 Template for Inventory of Activities

Department /Function:			**Head:**			**Date:**		
Role: I **Objective:**			**Role: 2** **Objective:**			**Role: 3** **Objective:**		
Id	Activity Name	% of Time Spent	Id	Activity Name	% of Time Spent	Id	Activity Name	% of Time Spent
Observations:			Observations:			Observations:		

Step 2: Create inventory for all the activities

The input of this can be obtained from Table 4.7. above. Ensure that each of the activities done is listed and the corresponding time spent on each is mentioned. Look at the job description of each and ascertain their function and the time required to perform them. If a job description is not available, get an idea of the role from the functional head. This is not the best option but till the job description is in place, we can adopt this approach. It is imperative to mention the observations at the end of each role for subsequent analysis/action. It should be noted that for managerial roles an exact time and motion cannot be done. For managerial roles one has to assess an approximate time to do the activity.

Table 4.8 Template for Inventory Activities (filled)

Function: *Internal Consulting*			**Head:** *Deb Cooper*			**Date:** *June 27, 2008*		
Role: *Engagement Manager*			**Role:** *Capability Building Leader*			**Role:** *Practice Leader*		
Objective: *Engage business units to adopt practices of quality for business improvement*			**Objective:** *Create competent resources within business units so that they can carry out improvement without external help*			**Objective:** *Develop quality practices for leveraging for business improvement*		
Id	Activity Name	% of Time Spent	Id	Activity Name	% of Time Spent	Id	Activity Name	% of Time Spent
	Business Engagement	*30%*		*Capability Strategy*	*20%*		*Practice Development*	*30%*
	Manage Project Execution	*30%*		*Capability Execution*	*25%*		*Knowledge Scanning*	*10%*
	Practice Development	*20%*		*Business Engagement*	*40%*		*Manage Project Execution*	*30%*
	Follow Up with Back Office	*20%*		*Follow Up with Back Office*	*15%*		*Capability*	*30%*
Observations: *Question why time is being spent on Follow-Up. Time spent on Practice Development is high. Are there issues with the Practice Leader? Time spent on business engagement is quite less.*			**Observations:** *Time spent on capability execution is less. Why does the person need to spend time on business engagement? Follow-up should be reduced or eliminated.*			**Observations:** *Why is the individual spending time to manage project and capability execution? The time being spent on knowledge scan is pretty less. Work towards eliminating the role overlaps.*		

Table 4.8 on the previous page is an example of a few roles in an internal consulting function of a bank which underwent a Lean process. For each of the observations get into the root causes and work towards eliminating them. However, for front liners, the approach has to be much more detailed and has been discussed in Lesson 3.

Leaning Duplicate Functions

Over a period of time similar functions/departments get created within the organization. During one of my Lean engagements in a services business I saw that despite having a customer-services call centre for the organization, a branch office had put in place a team which worked on customer queries. This was a clear example of a duplicate office wherein a call centre had been created within a bank branch, which was not required. The reason for this was to cover any just-in-case scenarios.

This is a big problem especially in large organizations wherein over a period of time functions get duplicated, only to add to costs and hide inefficiencies. To address such a problem a template such as the one showed in Table 4.9 below can be used.

Table 4.9 Template for Inefficiency Assessment

Function:			**Objective:**					
Business:			**Business:**			**Business:**		
Geo-1	Geo-2	Geo-3	Geo-1	Geo-2	Geo-3	Geo-1	Geo-2	Geo-3

(geo stands for geographies).

Table 4.10 shows an example of an assessment for functional redundancies in an organization. As you can see, over a period of time redundancies have set in.

Table 4.10 Assessment of Functional Redundancies

Function: *Human Resource*			**Objective:** *To ascertain the functional redundancies in a financial services organization.*				
Business: *Retail Banking*			**Business:** *Corporate Banking*		**Business:** *SME Banking*		
Asia	*Europe*	*Americas*	*Asia*	*Europe*	*Asia*	*Europe*	*Americas*
India (2000/ 15000)	*UK (70/ 2000)*	*Toronto (120/ 5000)*	*India (20/500)*	*UK (5/50)*	*India (45/ 1000)*	*UK (18/ 200)*	*Canada (5/200)*
Singapore (50/ 1000)	*Germany (10/ 100)*	*Argentina (2/20)*	*Singapore (5/50)*	*Germany (5/20)*			*Brazil (5/100)*
Hong Kong (20/550)	*Nordics (5/100)*	*Peru (55/1000)*			*Hong Kong (50/ 5000)*		
			It did not operate in Corporate Banking space in the Americas				

(The figures in the numerator show the HR employees and the ones in the denominator show the total number of employees).

As you see from the Table 4.10, there is something clearly amiss. The ratio of HR professionals to total employees varies across geographies and does not follow a uniform trend. On investigating, dissonances were found not only in numbers but also levels. This was a case of an organization which had grown inorganically and inherited varied practices from its lineage.

Key Takeaways

- While leaning processes, we should not forget that many inefficiencies hide within the functional crevices of the organization.
- For all key roles in the company, ascertain the time spent on real value addition–this should be looked at by leaders on a regular basis.
- Teach all HR professionals to look at roles from a Lean lens.
- Optimizing the activities of the key roles can radically enhance organizational productivity.

Lesson 41

White Spaces can be Potential Opportunities for Lean Application

Geary A. Rummler and Alan P. Brache gave us the concept of white spaces in 1991. White spaces are the areas between the boxes in an organization chart or the areas between different functions which do not have ownership. According to Rummler and Brache, there are maximum opportunities for improvement in these places as they do not have any ownership and efforts made fall between the cracks. This concept is very relevant in the implementation of Lean in an organization.

From a Lean perspective, each of these spaces is a hatchery of wasteful activities and provides a great opportunity for operational excellence. To ascertain Lean opportunities in an organization, it is a good idea to list all the white spaces in the company. The larger the number of white spaces in the company, the greater the opportunity for Lean. Each of these is a haven for hidden factories, which are on nobody's radar. In our discussions we will also look at these issues. The following are a few things which could be symptomatic of potential white spaces in the company:

- Issues having no ownership,
- Orphan infrastructure/equipments/capital items,
- Headless functions,
- Locations/geographies/branches without a leader,
- Time spent in coordinating.

White Spaces in processes

A handy approach to finding out white spaces in a process is to break a core process into broad components and then look for their owners (Figure 4.3 on the facing page). Components without ownership are a clear opportunity for action. Installing process ownership is probably the first step towards managing these white spaces.

Strategic Ownership Matrix

Given the issues of ownership, it helps to inventorize all the key issues impacting the organization. So how does one go about doing so? The three-step approach shown on the next page can help:

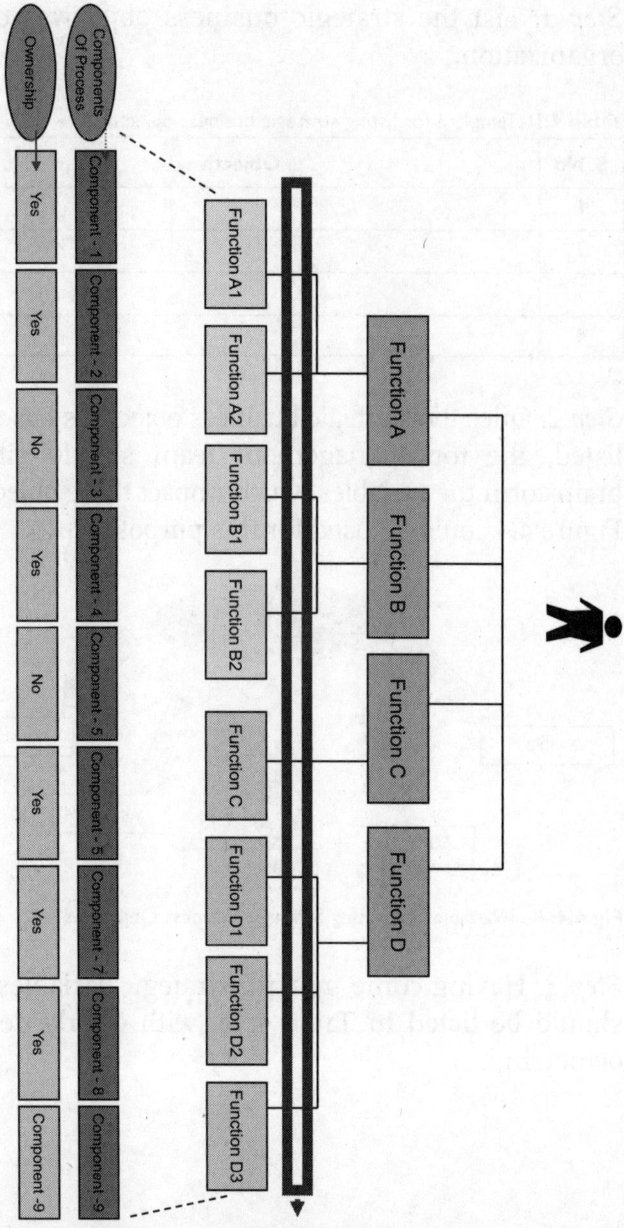

Fig 4.3: Finding White Spaces in Processes

Step 1: List the strategic business objectives of the organization.

Table 4.11 Template for listing strategic business objectives

S. No	Objective
1	
2	
3	
4	

Step 2: Once the strategic business objectives have been listed, the top management team should sit and brainstorm the variables which impact these objectives. Figure 4.4 could be used for this purpose.

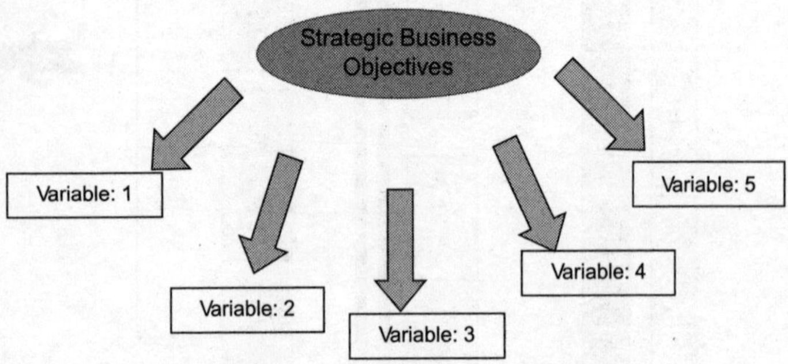

Fig 4.4: Key Variables Impacting Strategic Business Objectives

Step 3: Having come up with strategic variables they should be listed in Table 4.12, with clearly defined ownership.

Table 4.12 Template for Strategic Business Objectives

Strategic Business Objective (SBO)	Key Variables Impacting the SBO	Owner	Stand-in

Though this matrix may not drive ownership of all issues in the organization, it can at least ensure that the issues impacting the strategic business objectives are taken care of.

Key Takeaways

- White spaces can tacitly take an organization down the performance spiral.
- White spaces are hatcheries for waste and opportunities for Lean application.
- Regularly look for white spaces within the organizational crevices.
- Driving ownership is the first step to remove white spaces.

Lesson 42

Distribute and Optimize Capacity Via Multi-Skilling

A key solution implemented during Lean interventions is multi-skilling, or cross-training of employees. Multi-skilling is done to achieve the following objectives:

- Create capacities,
- Manage peaks in demand/volumes,
- Distribute capacity,
- Create competency,
- Bring the need for capability building of process associates to the agenda of top management,
- Optimize the process,
- Build process flexibility and resilience which helps to manage emergencies and exigencies.

So how does one go about multi-skilling in a service context? The following is an approach which I have found quite useful:

Step 1: Process Selection

Select a process or a process family or a set of processes based on a certain criteria. It could be based on volume, business objective or cost.

Step 2: Objective Identification

Define the objective of the process/business which is being targeted for multi-skilling. Look at all the business objectives that it needs to accomplish. Specifically look at the productivity numbers which are being targeted.

Step 3: Volume Dissection

Do a thorough demand analysis. Look at volumes and the trend of customer requirements. Get data on the following:

- Average Demand
- Peak Demand

Step 4: Existing Numbers

Take stock of the existing manpower and sections where we would like to improve productivity.

Step 5: Process Deconstruction

Break the processes into activities and tasks (see Table 4.13 on the next page).

Please note that in each of the activities there could be large number of tasks for individuals to work on.

Table 4.13 Template for Strategic Ownership Matrix

Process	Activity	Tasks
Process I	Activity A	Task I Task II
	Activity B	Task I Task II Task III
	Activity C	Task I
Process 2	Activity A	Task I Task II

Step 6: Activity Prioritization

Among all the activities, further prioritize the activities that you may like to take in Step 1. Ideally all the activities in the selected process/process family should be looked at for multi-skilling, but sometimes that may not be possible due to resource constraints. As an illustration, please go through Table 4.14 which provides an example of activity prioritization for multi-skilling on a scale of importance from 1 to 10.

Table 4.14 Example of Activity Prioritization in Multi-skilling

Process	Activity	Importance
Account Opening Process	*Mailing Room*	1
	In-warding	3
	Verification	10
	Risk Assessment	7
	Scanning	10
	Processing	3

(Importance can be based on business objectives productivity, customers etc.)

Step 7: Skill Competency Mapping

Map the existing skill levels of all employees and grade their competencies as shown in Table 4.15.

Table 4.15 Gradation of Skills

Grade	Details
Novice	Un-initiated and yet to be exposed to the activity/task
Under-study	Currently undergoing training or has just completed training and started implementing it. Needs continual supervision.
Practicing	Can independently do the activity and does not require supervision
Expert	Has mastered the activity and can train others

Step 8: Implementation Plan

Put in place an implementation plan. Ensure that the progress is reviewed by a senior leader on a regular basis. Given the organic nature of the cross-training, it may make sense to roll out it in phases. The broad approach to be followed here is as follows:

Phase 1: Focus on +1 and −1. This is about cross-training individuals on skills preceding and succeeding a particular activity in a process. This should happen in a period of three months.

Phase 2: Focus on cross-training of all associates within value stream/business/operational silos. This could happen in a period of six to twelve months.

Phase 3: Focus on cross-training of relevant associates in at least three core processes or process loops in a selected value stream. This should take a time frame of 12 to 18 months.

Phase 4: In this phase look at cross-training of all relevant associates in all core processes/process-loops. This should take a time-frame of 18 to 24 months.

Step 9: Install Metrics

To ascertain ongoing performance a few metrics should be put in place which should be tracked through a dashboard (See Table 4.16).

Table 4.16 Dashboard for Tracking Multi-skilling

Metrics	Measurement Output		
	Percentage	Number	Time
Number and Percentage of associates multi-skilled in a process	✓	✓	
Number and Percentage of members equipped on +1 to −1	✓	✓	
Number and Percentage of core processes which have multi-skilled associates	✓	✓	
Time taken to get the new process up with the cross-trained resources			✓
Time taken to allow a process to get operational with the multi-skilled resources			✓

Remember, cross-training takes time and can happen when it is driven strategically. Do not expect quick results. You have to be patient and work at it. It's only then that you will see it as being a lever for business enhancement.

Key Takeaways

- Multi-skilling is one of most under-utilized tools for business improvement. Leverage it to deliver results over a period of time.
- Multi-skilling takes time and the organization should be patient.
- Multi-skilling should be driven by a senior leader in the organization.
- To begin with, focus on +1 to -1 multi-skilling.
- Multi-skilling helps to prepare an organization for unexpected scenarios.

Lesson 43

Is Your Cross Selling Inefficienly Ineffective?

Cross-selling refers to the approach wherein you try and sell more products or services to your customer. It is often a big focus of organizations. Having closely watched a large number of cross-selling processes in services organizations, I have seen how companies inadvertently generate waste, which can easily be avoided.

In their enthusiasm to increase business volume, organizations often implement a large number of cross-selling goals around their products or services. The belief here is that an increase in the company's share of the customer's wallet will lead to a long and profitable relationship with them. While this assumption may not be wrong, the existing approach for cross-selling could lead to sub-optimal results.

Companies share their cross-sell figures with analysts and celebrate successes around it. It is quite possible that we may be celebrating something which may not really be an achievement at all. While the volumes may be going up, demonstrating penetration and increase in market-share, the customer requirements may not really have been met. This is where Lean principles come into play. Figure 4.5 shows the typical approach to cross-selling followed by companies. As you can see, the approach is quite inwardly focused. The focus is to peddle what is available and not really on what the customer values.

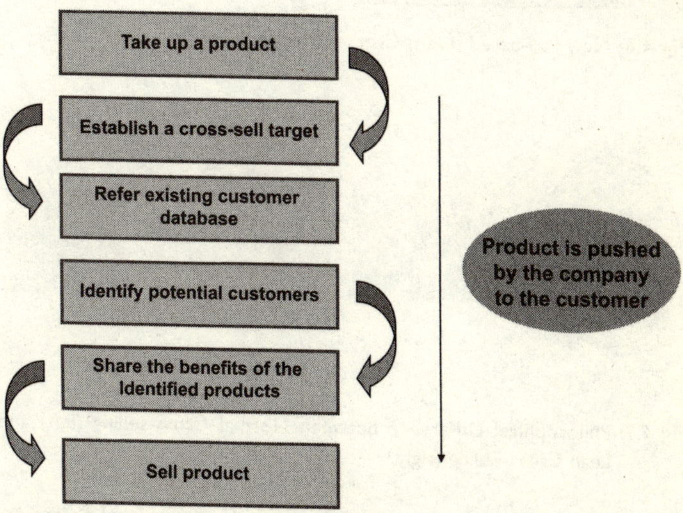

Fig 4.5: Typical Push-based Cross-sell Process

Re-design the process keeping in mind the voice of customer and what he or she values. Create a process wherein the products get pulled by the customer. The new pull-based process is shown in Figure 4.6. The conceptual approach for this is explained in Figure 4.7.

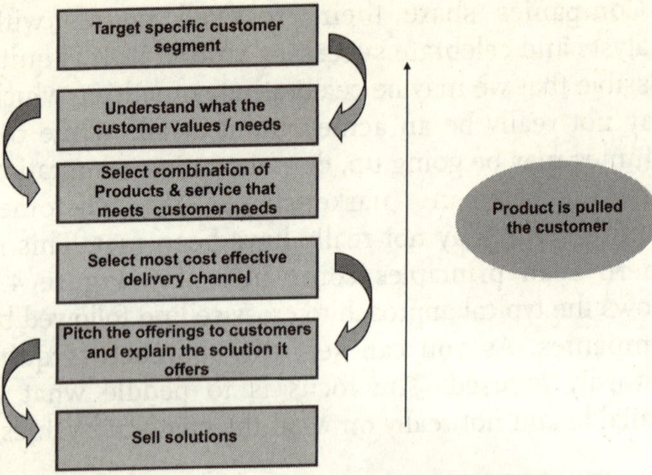

Fig 4.6: New Pull-based (Lean) Cross-sell Process

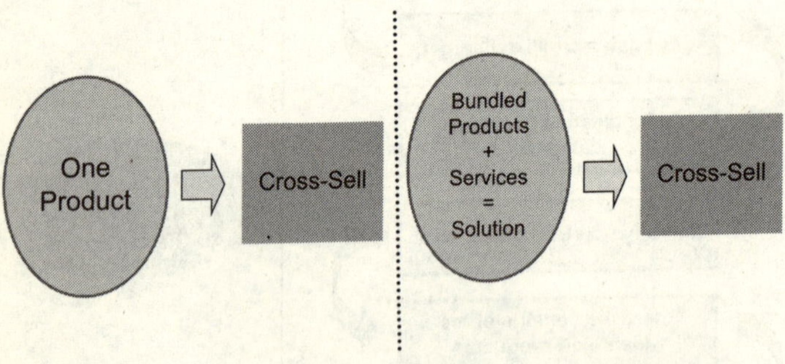

Fig 4.7: Philosophical Difference between Normal Cross-selling (left) and Lean Cross-selling (right)

The objective of a Lean intervention should be to enhance cross-sale's effectiveness in an efficient manner. To put it simply, this is about expanding sales volume at minimal cost with the existing customers. However, there is a need to ensure that the needs of the customers are met. There has to be a positive co-relationship between cross-sale and actual fulfillment of customer needs.

The key traits of the new Lean cross process are:

- The organization provides a solution to a customer need (remember, Lean is about solving the customer's problems),
- The solution gets pulled by the customer instead of being pushed by the company,
- The focus is not just on the product but also on the associated services,
- Sales colleagues associated with the product are not just salesmen but have been trained on multiple products and solution selling,
- Huge focus on assessing what the customer needs,
- Focus on mutual value adds—the customer gets what s/he wants while it is economically rewarding for the company.

A Lean cross-sell process will not only increase the share of the wallet but also market share. The former is about making the same customer spend more on products or services from the company, while the latter is about getting a larger number of customers. When a company follows the Lean cross-sell process, the overall cost of ownership goes down.

Key Takeaways
■ A Lean cross-sell process is economically rewarding to both the customer as well as to the company. ■ Just cross-selling a product does not mean that the customer's requirement is being met. ■ Begin your cross-sales by understanding what solution the customer is seeking. ■ A Lean cross-sell process should not only be highly effective but also cost least to the company.

Lesson 44

INSTILL AN ENTERPRISE-WIDE PROBLEM-SOLVING PROCESS

Leaders and managers are essentially hired to solve business problems. However, companies do not invest sufficiently to develop this skill. A lot of money is spent on competency development programmes, but very little is invested on equipping teams on problem-solving skills.

A key element to building a Lean culture is to make everyone in the company practice PDCA. So what is PDCA? It stands for Plan-Do-Check-Act. The components of PDCA are shown in Table 4.17.

Table 4.17 Details of PDCA

P	Plan	Plan a change process
D	Do	Carry out the required change on a small scale
C	Check	Review the results, What went right? What went wrong? What were the learnings?
A	Act	Take action based on the results. If the results are successful, scale up the change. If it did not work, begin the cycle again.

The PDCA cycle was originally conceived of by Walter Shewhart and later adopted by William Edward Deming, who is often referred to as the father of modern quality management. Deming referred to it as the Shewhart cycle but the PDCA cycle is now often known as the Deming's Wheel or Deming's Cycle (Figure 4.8).

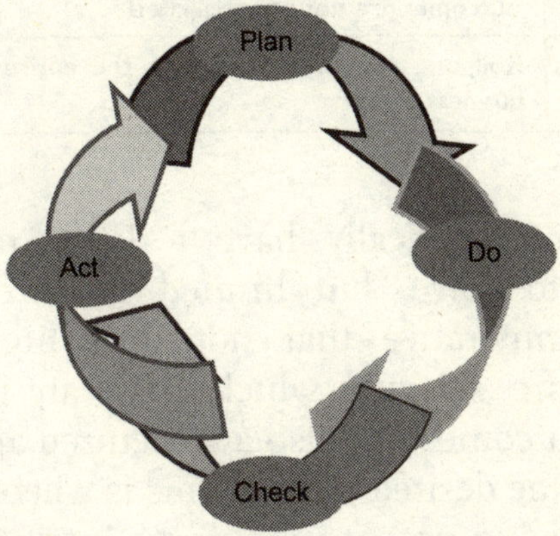

Fig 4.8: The PDCA Cycle

The universal nature of the PDCA cycle is such that it can be applied to any type of problem irrespective of the industry, company or context. It can be used for any change process. To drive continuous improvement, the PDCA process has to be repeated again and again.

To see how PDCA thinking superimposes with problem solving, let us refer to Table 4.18 on the next page.

Table 4.18 PDCA and Problem Solving

P	Plan	Identify the problem. Define it clearly. Collect relevant data. Predict the expected change from the project. Brainstorm all possible root causes. Propose solutions. Prepare a plan for implementation.
D	Do	Go ahead and implement the solutions. It is done with the objective to test the hypothesis of the solutions.
C	Check	Gather performance data on the solutions that have been implemented. Capture the learnings. Investigate if the outcomes are not as anticipated.
A	Act	Roll out the solutions across the entire organization/ business system

Organizations typically have a large number of problems to solve, but limited resources. So, it becomes imperative that not only high priority problems are selected which have an impact on business outcomes but also a structured approach is used to get the desired results. This is where a generic problem-solving process should be institutionalized across the organization so that it can be used by all levels in different contexts. If there are too many problem-solving approaches floating around in the company, employees can get confused about which method to adopt in what situation. I always believe that the problem solving approach has to be simple so that all and sundry in the company can use it. As mentioned in Lesson 5, let the organization have capabilities in multiple methodologies and tools, but for solving they should use a generic approach. While I do endorse the PDCA approach for solving problems, my personal favourite approach is the A3 structure which was discussed in Lesson 32 and is also based on the PDCA philosphy. I have seen the A3 structure is highly suited to solving problems faced in varied service settings. Organizations can also adopt problem-solving methods such as DMAIC (Define-Measure-Analyse-Improve-Control).

Educating teams on this problem-solving process cannot just be confined to middle and front-liners, but it also has to be used by top management. A generic problem-solving approach helps teams to emerge from fire-fighting to a structured approach to address workplace issues. Jeffrey Liker and Michael Hoseus in their book *Toyota Culture: The Heart and Soul of the Toyota Way*, talk about Toyota's problem-solving method called Toyota Business Practices which was launched in 2005 in the USA (Figure 4.9).

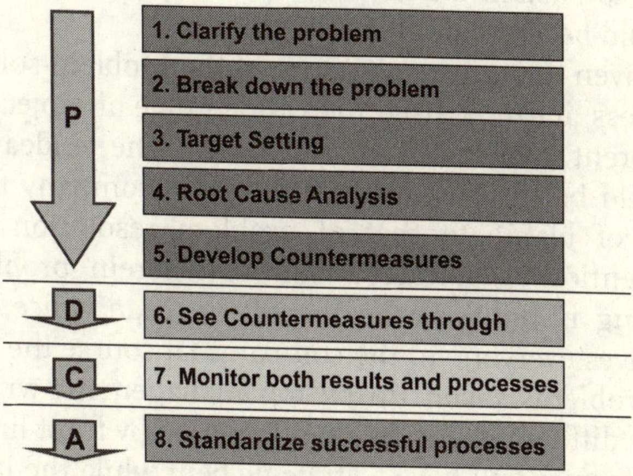

Fig 4.9: Toyota Business Practices
Adopted from: *Toyota Culture: The Heart and Soul of the Toyota Way*, Jeffrey K Liker and Michael Hoseus (McGraw-Hill, 2008).

Instilling a problem-solving culture results in the teams involved improving their workplace and also contributing towards business betterment. This can be quite satisfying for the employees, as they feel quite good about being able to contribute to the issues which their leaders want to solve. Organizations need to shun their focus on tools and really get into creating capabilities, allowing employees to solve their day-to-day problems.

All employees in the company should be taught the art of problem-solving. Every new entrant in the company, across the hierarchy, needs to undergo this training. While reviewing outcomes of projects, the leaders should not only look at the results but also the process followed. In fact, if someone comes up with a result without following the proper process, they should treat it as a blind-folded walk. As a matter of fact, to sustain a Lean fabric, daily problem-solving should be a way of life.

Given the universal nature of the problem-solving process, it can be used for a wide range of projects in different contexts and functions. The endeavour should be to shift the culture of the company from that of blame to that of problem resolution and prevention. Inculcate a culture wherein problem-solving is not just the job of the Lean office, but involves everyone in the company. Of course the type of problems taken up by top management will be quite different from the ones taken up by front-liners. The former will have a strategic bent while the latter will be very tactical in nature. However, the approach that they will follow will be the same.

Key Takeaways

- Mastering the art of understanding the cause and effect relationship in organizational problems is critical to building a fabric of Lean thinking in the company.
- The entire company should have a common problem-solving approach.
- To achieve this, educate all employees across hierarchies on problem-solving techniques
- Senior leaders should walk the talk and use the problem-solving approach for both strategic and tactical problems.
- Creating a problem-solving culture should be a key focus area of the Lean office.

Lesson 45

Only Focussing on a Good Service Recovery Process can be Quite Myopic

Many customer service professionals would be astonished at this lesson. Their view would be: how can we have a service organization and not talk about the service recovery process? So much has been written on the service recovery process and how it can help to get back customers. Complaint handling and service recovery go hand in hand and are looked at as enablers for customer retention. Research has shown that customers whose concerns are resolved quickly are more likely to be loyal to the company. Efficient service recovery helps to elevate the organization's capacity to maintain effective customer relationships. Service recovery also provides an opportunity to the organization to further its business by cross-selling or up-selling its products and services.

It is not that I am against service recovery processes. They are required and must be there in all businesses. If customers have problems, the onus is on the company to make the required corrections so that customers can be retained. My discomfort is not with the service recovery processes, but with the goal of an organization to build good service recovery processes and protocol.

As Lean practitioners we should realize that service recovery is about addressing the symptoms and not getting into the root cause. We do not realize that just focusing on service recovery is associated with one of the following:

1. It adds to unnecessary costs. We do not realize that installing service recovery protocols means putting in place an infrastructure to manage it.
2. If we just focus on service recovery, we could be forgetting to prevent the defects which could be happening in the process.

So, what should be the approach to this whole issue in an organization on a Lean journey? The following are a few pointers which should always be kept in mind:

- Make defect prevention the goal of a process,
- Do everything in the process for better customer engagement,
- Design processes which ensure the output (product/service) is flawless,
- Focus on providing such impeccable service that customers do not come back to you with their problems,

- Provide world-class training and capability development programs,
- Provide proactive service instead of reactive,
- Make everyone in the company own service, not just the customer-services department,
- Create an engaging service that customers enjoy.

Once the above have been done, the company should put in place a world-class and robust service recovery process which helps to manage the service failures. This process should be so good that even if the customer is peeved, he will decide not only to stay with the company but also advocate others to do the same.

However, it would be suicidal for an organization to just focus on building service recovery process and not focus on designing processes and hiring people who can create a flawless product and service. To see if companies are getting this concept right, companies should keep their eye on the metrics shown in Table 4.19.

Table 4.19 Metrics for Service Recovery

Metrics
Number of products or service delivered right first time
Percentage of products or service delivered right first time
Number of service recoveries
Percentage of service recoveries

Key Takeaways

- Just focusing on service recovery process, without an eye on designing and managing processes and products (or service) can be suicidal,
- Lean is about creating great processes and products, and scripting recovery protocols for failures which are rare and not a norm.
- The organization should have a well-designed approach to service recovery
- It is imperative that an organization monitor the number of service recoveries.
- They should go down over a period of time.

Lesson 46

Too Many MIS Reports can make Business Ineffective

We all know that Management Information Systems are a mechanism for collecting, processing, storing and disseminating data in the form of information to facilitate the functioning of the management and allow proper decision making.

However, does your company have the problem of too many management information system (MIS) reports? Do reports get generated by every function and department? Do MIS reports get generated at the drop of a hat, or with every change in leadership? Are reports prepared, but no one looks at them? All these are symptoms of deep waste in the organization. Multiple MIS Reports generate a large number of problems in the organization. Not only do they increase waste but also have knock-on effects, leading to:

- Huge confusion on definitions/interpretations,
- Energies wasted in defending reports/holding one's turf,
- Man-hours wasted in preparing reports that have little value,
- IT storage space wasted to store data which is of no relevance,
- Data sources being questioned and issues raised about data integrity,
- Faulty decision making.

So how does one go about resolving this problem? This can be effectively done following the approach listed in Table 4.20. Do a detailed dissection through the Lean prism and populate this template.

Table 4.20 MIS Report Rationalization

Steps	Details
Inventorize	List all the MIS Reports using the templates shown in Table 4.21.
Stop	Stop MIS reports being generated by all and sundry. This requires a mandate from the top management.
Define	Define the objectives and requirements of a MIS report by all levels of the organization.
Own	Co-opt a team which will have the responsibility of all MIS requirements of the company.
Detail	Detail exactly what MIS reports will and will not contain.
Implement	Implement the detailed new structure for MIS reporting.
Review	Install a regime of regular reviews of MIS reports and their relevance.

Table 4.21: Inventorization and Analysis of MIS Reports

Business Unit	Function	Departments (Within Function)	No of MIS reports produced	List of MIS Reports	Objective of Report	Target Audience of the Report	Who produces the Report	Man Hours Required	Areas covered in the Report	Remarks

The main reason why organizations get inundated with MIS reports is because there is no ownership for them as a whole. This is not given due importance and looked at as unimportant to a company's success. Make a team responsible for all the MIS reports for the company. If there are too many owners, the chances of errors and inaccuracies are imminent. A MIS Report should always be strategically aligned and should be designed in such a manner that it is relevant to the user. Stop all MIS reports being generated by individual workplace owners. Ensure that all data used for MIS come from a single source. Both these issues have to be audited regularly by team members. However, let there be sufficient flexibility to create newer forms of reports without really tinkering with the data source.

Issues pertaining to MIS reports can generate many inefficiencies in business which must be avoided at all costs. I would recommend that companies have an IT system for MIS which can be used enterprise-wide. Put a ban on usage of isolated spread sheets to generate reports, and insist on a template being followed for optimum data collection and collation. Let a senior leader in the company also take ownership of all MIS reports so that they are controlled and managed as required.

Key Takeaways

- MIS reports have to be produced and used effectively or they can consume a large amount of organizational bandwidth and even result in faulty decisions.
- Multiple MIS reports often indicate a lack of belief in the existing reporting system.
- While looking at MIS reports do not forget issues related to data integrity and ownership.
- An organization should have a single source for all MIS reports.
- Inadequacies in MIS reporting can make leaders take incorrect decisions.

Lesson 47

Use Sales Partners to Build Relationships

Many service organizations employ sales partners to whom they outsource their sales processes. The purpose with which such entities are appointed is to drive sales to meet targets. While there is nothing wrong with gunning to achieve sales targets, the mindset and approach behind it is incorrect. The whole engagement is driven by a push mindset where the intent is to somehow sell (read: push) the product or service to the customer. As a result, products or services are often dumped on customers whether they want them or not. This leads to wrong selling, customer dissatisfaction and creates the impression of an overbearing organization.

The typical impact of push-based selling by partners leads to the following inefficiencies:

- Low conversion ratio,
- High customer attrition rate,
- Problems of incomplete applications leading them to go back and forth,
- Focus on completing the transaction at any cost,
- Instances of wrong selling of products and services,
- Little effort to understand what the customer really needs,
- Customers defect after some time or after experiencing the first product/service.

In an organization pursuing Lean, this approach has to change. Push-based selling has to metamorphose into Pull-based selling. This will happen when the company creates an environment in which customers come back, demanding more. This, in turn, happens when the role of the sales-partner changes from being a peddler of products and services to that of being a relationship creator. Positions such as Direct Sales Agency, Direct Marketing Agency or Distribution Partners have to undergo a change and should be re-designated as Customer Relationship Agency, relationship management partners or strategic partners. This is not easy and will require the entire leadership to look at these entities differently and the way their performances are managed. The profile of the individuals who work for these entities also has to be different. These entities need to be relationship-associates and just not sales-associates. The changes in the roles of these business gathering entities is summarized in Figure 4.10 on the facing page.

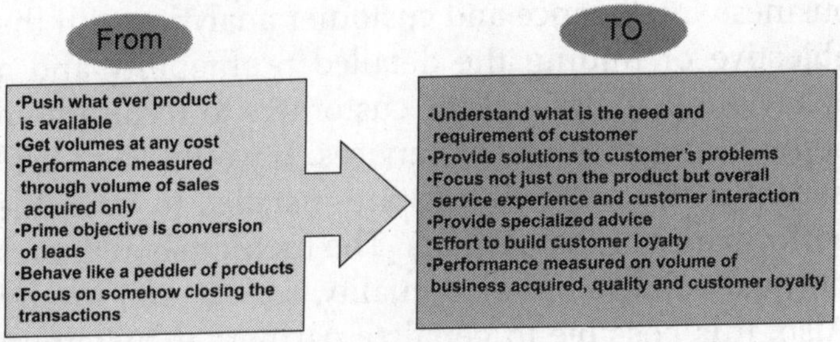

Fig 4.10: Role of Sales Partners in a Company Instilling Lean thinking

The purpose is to build a relationship that creates pull among customers to buy the company's product or service. The focus should be to achieve relationship primacy by demonstrating that they care for customers and provide them with products or service that is relevant to them. Remember, this will happen when customer relationship management is treated as a strategic priority.

The endeavour should be to target customer loyalty and hence get a larger share of the customer's wallet. This would require the company to invest in training for the partners, so that they are equipped to align customer requirements and needs with the right products. The focus of the partners should not be on just the specific transaction, but on creating a sense of comfort with the customer so that s/he returns with repeat business. Of course, all these would require selecting the right partners, who have been closely scrutinized before appointment. After getting them on board, not only is it necessary to equip their teams with right skills, but also to embed robust processes.

Yes, the partners would have to have the relevant technology-enabled infrastructure. This is required for business intelligence and customer analytics with the objective of finding the detailed profitability and a behavioural analysis of the customers to recommend better-fitting products or services. It would be critical here that the right metrics are installed to track the performance of the partners. The metrics should track not just volume but also quality, service and loyalty. Also, it is possible to penalize partners if customers defect within 90 days of acquisition.

A senior manager in the sales function should manage all these partners so that they are effective and efficient for the company. We may not realize it, but gaps in the partner relationship can create a lot of tacit inefficiencies which can clearly be avoided.

Key Takeaways
■ The biggest impact of push-based-selling is low conversion ratios and dissatisfied customers. ■ Involve your sales-partners in the Lean journey. ■ The compensation of sales-partners should be threaded with volume, quality, service and loyalty. ■ Myopic and ineffective sales processes can quietly saddle the company with many inefficiencies and wastes.

Lesson 48

Practice Visual Management

A key aspect of Lean management is visual management. Visual management is an approach to creating an information-rich workplace, using visually-stimulating aids such as graphical displays, boards, symbols, electronic boards, digital boards, lights etc, with the objective of managing and controlling performance.

It is a proactive approach that translates critical information into visual forms which cannot be ignored. The important data of the company is converted to sensory stimulating information that can not only sustain current performance levels but also help to facilitate continual improvement. The larger objective of visual management is to drive operational excellence, cut wastes and enhance processes.

A good visual management system should enable teams working on the shop-floor to take real-time actions on processes. Within a short period of time, an individual walking around the process would be in a position to know what is going on in the process, the current process performance and what actions should be taken to ensure the products/services are right the first time.

The tools used for visual management are targeted towards the following types of information:

- Strategic Information
- Tactical Information

Table 4.22 demonstrates the difference between the two.

Table 4.22: Difference between Strategic and Tactical Visual Information

Strategic Visual Information	Tactical Visual Information
These are data that provide the strategic view of the company. They help the associates to get a larger picture of the firm's performance. This information includes strategic parameters such as volume, profits, operating income, costs etc.	These are visual tools used to manage the day-to-day operations of a workplace. This information includes metrics on various operating parameters such as process efficiency, people productivity, process lead times etc.

As far as possible, the visual management should be a low-cost solution. However, in service companies, technology is often leveraged to create solutions which may require investment in things such as digital dashboards. Whatever approach is used, it should make the processes and workplace transparent. The whole objective of visual management should be to make the workplace/process speak for itself.

So, how does one go about deploying a visual management plan? Lesson 33 has already provided a holistic approach. The only thing that needs to be remembered is that it should be relevant to the maturity of the Lean journey and the objective (visual management) that it should serve. This means that leaders need to have a comprehensive plan while creating an environment for the teams to develop it in an organic manner.

The question that often bothers us is: how do we know that a visual management system has been designed correctly? Teams put a lot of effort into installing visual management controls but are not sure if they have done all the right things. An instrument shown in Table 4.23 will help you to ascertain the quality of your visual management system.

Table 4.23 Deb's Instrument for Assessing Visual Management Effectiveness

Attributes of Visual Management System (VMS)	Score (1–5)
Has been designed and created by the employees of the workplace	
Echoes the health of the workplace: walking around the workplace clearly tells you what is happening there	
Is intuitive, which means that employees are able to take action just by looking at it	
Clearly tells the teams the standards that need to be met	
Facilitates quick recovery when processes go awry (i.e. defects get produced/correct processes are not followed)	
Guides and tells teams on what they need to do to accomplish their day-to-day jobs	

Table 4.23 – Deb's Instrument for Assessing Visual Management Effectiveness (*Continued*)

Attributes of Visual Management System (VMS)	Score (1–5)
Aids in identifying wastes/inefficiencies in the system	
Customer demand is visible to the process associates	
Product/service being processed gets pulled by the customer	
Is a low-cost solution and did not require any investment	
Helps to find abnormalities in the workplace	
Provides "real-time" information (read: metrics) on the workplace performance (includes people, process, resource utilization, production etc)	
Does not allow defective items to enter the next stage of the process	
Facilitates solution of day-to-day problems in the workplace	
Used by leaders to review progress on a regular basis	
Refreshed on a regular basis and teams proactively question and change it for their relevance	
Has a live workplace visual board which acts as an information centre wherein teams meet at least twice a day	

Score each of the parameters and see the health of your visual management system. The rating scale has been detailed in Table 4.24. The interpretation of the scores is given in Table 4.25.

Table 4.24 Ratings for Deb's Instrument

Rating	What does it mean?
5	This is best-in-class and an benchmark for all to emulate
4	This is very good and has been institutionalized across all teams
3	This is functioning but there is only partial adoption
2	This has been installed and awareness has been established
1	This has just been installed
0	This does not exist

Table 4.25 Interpretation of Scores for Deb's Instrument

Score	Interpretation
Above 75	World-class visual management system which drives workplace efficiency and continual improvement
55 – 74	The visual management system has begun to act like an engine for workplace improvement
35 – 54	The visual management system has been partially deployed
20 – 34	The visual management system has just been established
Less than 20	There is no visual management system existing in the company

Remember, a good visual management system has to be made with the involvement of teams. It has to be so engaging that it catalyzes teams into workplace improvement.

Key Takeaways

- Keep the visual management system simple. Let it not be something so complicated that it cannot be changed by the local teams.
- Visual management should capture both strategic and tactical information.
- As far as possible, use a low-cost solution for visual management.
- In a service context sometimes using information technology becomes imperative–do not think it is an un-Lean action.
- Use Deb's instrument to ascertain the effectiveness of visual management at least once in six months.

Lesson 49

A Little-known Law has Huge Powers to Drive Lean Solutions

There is a little-known law which has lots of application in Lean solutions. It is called Little's Law.

Derived by John Little at the MIT Sloan School of Management in 1961, this law has universal applicability to all types of business systems. All leaders and practitioners involved in Lean deployment should know this law very clearly and understand its application.

Little's Law states that the average number of works-in-progress in a stable system is equal to the completion rate multiplied by their average time in the system. This relationship is shown below:

Work-In-Progress = Throughput Time × Average Completion Rate

This relationship can also be shown as follows:

$$\text{Throughput Time} = \frac{\text{Work in Progress}}{\text{Completion Rate}} = \frac{\text{Work in Progress}}{\text{Input Rate}}$$

$$\frac{\text{Work in Progress}}{\text{Output Rate}}$$

To understand this better, let us look at a back-office process shop (Figure 4.11 on the facing page) where the mortgage application forms enter and exit at a constant rate of 100 files per day. If the average inventory of application forms at any given moment is 800 forms, we can use Little's Law to find the Throughput Time or the average time while the files are in the shop. Using the formula, the throughput time will be 8 days.

Let us see some real-life applications, which will demonstrate the power of Little's Law and how leaders can use it. Please refer to Table 4.26 below, and Tables 4.27 and 4.28 on the next page.

Table 4.26 Branch Teller

You are a running a retail bank branch. Let us talk about the tellers which are used by customers for transactions. On an average six customers are serviced every 20 minutes and there are 12 customers in the queue. The branch manager wants to know the average time a customer will spend in the line. We could use Little's Law to respond to the branch manager.
Here, the Work In Progress (WIP) is 12 customers
Rate at which customers get services = 6/ 20 = 0.3 customers
Average time for which customers will be in line = 12/0.3 = 40 minutes.
Yes, it takes 40 minutes to service the customers. The bank needs to do something about this before customers switch to other companies.

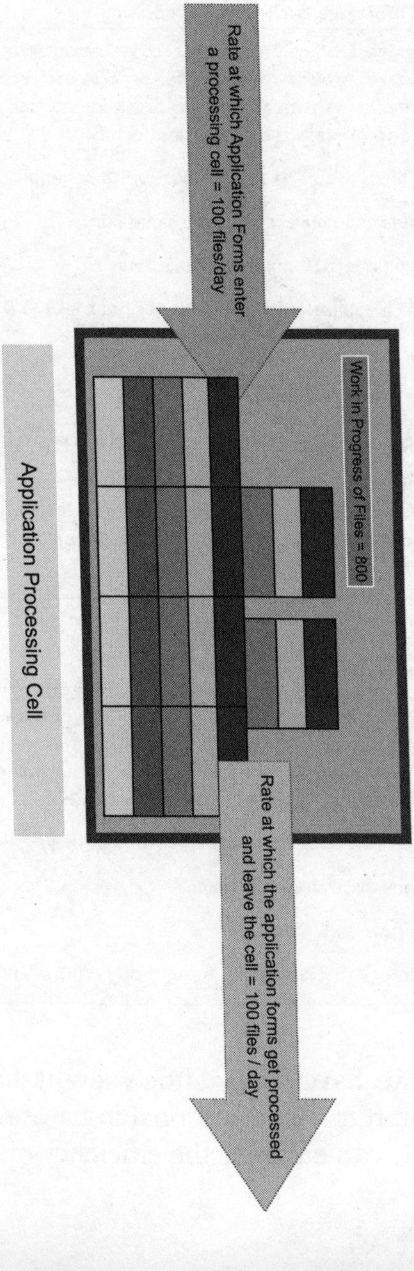

Fig 4.11: Back-Office Process Shop Functions

Table 4.27 Mortgage Back-Office Processing

A mortgage back-office processing receives on an average 320 applications per day. It takes around 30 minutes to process each application form. Each shift has nine hours with a one hour break in between. How many people are needed to process the application form?
In this problem, we need to find WIP which is people.
It is important to convert all in the same unit.
Throughput time is 30 minutes = 0.5 hour
Rate at which application is received per hour = 320/8 = 40/hour
WIP = Throughput Time × Completion Rate
WIP = 40 × 0 .5 = 20 people
Given the current throughput times, the processing requires 20 people.
It may be noted that as a part of Lean implementation, we may decide to improve the productivity of employees as a result of which more number of applications can be processed by the same people or we may decide to re-deploy the existing employees.

Table 4.28 Inventory in a Store

A mom-and-pop store sells 700 kg of chicken every week. The owner wants to ensure that the stock of chicken is never more than two days old. What quantity of chicken should the owner store to ensure that none of the inventory crosses the two-day threshold?
Rate at which chicken gets bought = 700 kg/7 days = 100 Kg/Day
Ensure all items have the same unit.
Throughput Time = 2 days.
Average Inventory that should be in the shop (WIP) = 100 × 2 = 200 Kg.

So, as we have seen, Little's law is has universal application. It is very directional in nature and using it successfully can enhance the efficiency of a company.

Key Takeaways

- Little's Law states that the average number of works-in-progress in a stable system is equal to the completion rate multiplied by their average time in the system.
- Little's Law is a simple law which has large number of intuitive applications. It is a must-know for all managers, leaders and change-agents involved in Lean transformation.
- Equip your leaders with various aspects of Little's Law application so that they know when and how it can be applied.

Lesson 50

Creating a Good Pull System can Take Time

The concept of pull is essentially about responding to the customer's demand. The objective of a Lean system should be to design such products or services which meet the changing needs of customers. The customer could be the end customer (also called the consumer or end-user) or even the next person in the process. The objective of a pull system should to provide the customer what is required, when it's required, at the price that the customer is willing to pay.

Simply put, the principle in pull is about not producing anything before the next step in the process it. In a larger scheme of things, pull is about orchestrating with all stakeholders in the process such as vendors, outsourced partners etc; with an objective to providing the customer a solution to the problems, conveniently and at the right price. Examples of pull systems are:

- Dell will not build a computer till you order one.
- Cheque books being made after a customer requests them through the internet.
- *Kanban* cards trigger stationery orders in an office.
- Supermarkets not storing more than what is required and replenishing items on a daily basis.
- Music companies not pushing their products (songs in CDs) to retail shelves but customers pulling their desired content from Amazon, Netflix, etc.
- Rather than pushing individuals into class rooms, companies have created a large amount of e-learning content which can be accessed by employees when needed (clearly a pull-based approach).

However, creating a pull system which connects the entire end-to-end process can take time. One has to go step-by-step. This becomes especially difficult when processes are large and cut across geographies. In such a case it is recommended to break the processes into sub-processes and then connect them through a pull system. The first step should be to streamline and create a continuous flow in the sub-processes. This would entail removing bottlenecks from these processes and ensuring that the items that are being processed move without any hurdle. Having smoothened the sub-processes, the focus should be in connecting these together through a pull system (Figure 4.12).

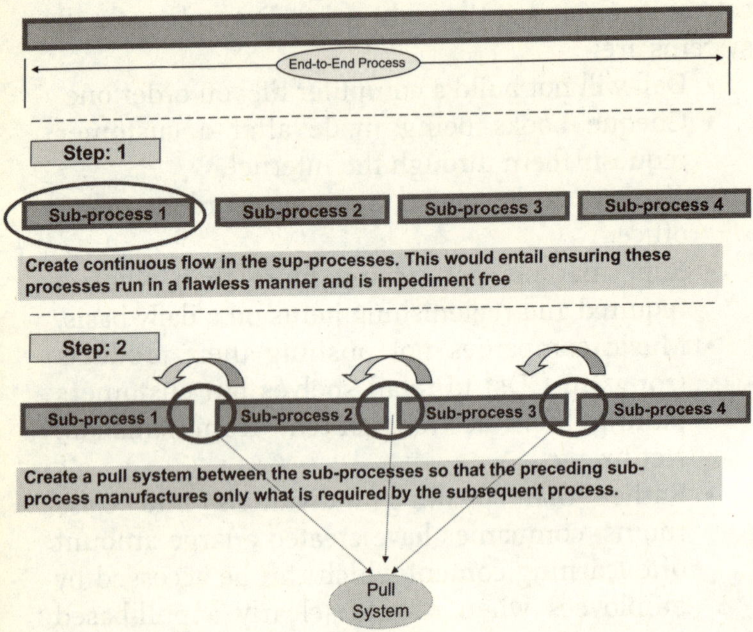

Fig 4.12: Step-wise Approach to Creating a Pull System

In an ideal case, you would like the entire end-to-end process to have a continuous flow. But in real life you will, in all likelihood, have to create a hybrid model which has both pull and push concepts.

A push system assumes customers as mute spectators who will accept whatever you offer them. In a pull system a platform is created so that resources can come in to provide customers what they need, when they need and in the quantity they need. In a pull model, distributed resources come together to work on the unanticipated needs of the customer. The platform in a pull system should be able to provide for the diverse needs of customers. A push system comprises tightly coupled modules which function in a pre-defined sequence. A pull system contains loosely coupled modules which are actually designed to build flexibility.

These modules could be sub-processes, physical entities, vendors etc. Based on the customer requirements which could often be unanticipated, these modules come together to create the product or service. An important dimension of a pull system in a service context is distributed communities coming together to find innovative ways to solve customer's problems. One of the objectives of Lean transformation is to make sure that there is an impeccable relationship among the various parties in the network.

Key Takeaways
■ Pull systems are about providing customers whatever is required, when required and at the right price. ■ As product types proliferate, a pull system provides an effective mechanism to provide the customer whatever is required. ■ A pull system is managed and triggered by a Kanban or a signal. ■ In a pull system, the endeavor should be to create an impeccable relationship among the various parties involved in the process. ■ Creating a pull system in a service context can be quite demanding and may require the help of information technology.

Lesson 51

Use Little's Law to Create Pull in Transaction Processing

Little's Law can come in very handy to create pull within processing cells. To create pull, the objective of a cell should be to maintain a stipulated WIP (also called calculated threshold) which has been arrived at based on the desired standard lead times and the processing (completion) rate. The endeavour should be to maintain the calculated WIP and restrict entry of items till the WIP in the cell reduces to below the calculated threshold. To explain this point, let us look at a credit processing cell in auto finance. The following are some of the process data:

- Average rate at which the application forms get processed per day = 100 (i.e. on an average 100 files get processed each day by this cell).

- Standard Throughput time with which the application forms need to get processed = 12 hours (0.5 days).

Let us use Little's Law to find out the desired WIP to ensure that the throughput time of 12 hours (0.5 days) is maintained. We go ahead and incorporate the data into the formula of Little's Law, which is as follows:

$$\textbf{0.5 days} = \frac{\textbf{Desired Work in Progress}}{\textbf{100 application forms/day}}$$

Required Work in Progress in the Cell = 50 application forms

This means in order to meet the Throughput Time of 0.5 days at any given moment of time, the average WIP in the Cell should be 50 application forms. The team should put into place a mechanism to ensure additional application forms do not enter the cell till the number of WIPs in the cell comes down to 49. This can be achieved by an electronic signal as shown in Figure 4.13 on the next page. The cell pulls in new entries only when the inventory falls to 49 as the runner replenishes it.

There are practitioners who say that pull in a Lean context is not possible. They are not correct. There are number of ways by which pull can be created in a service context. This example is just one of them.

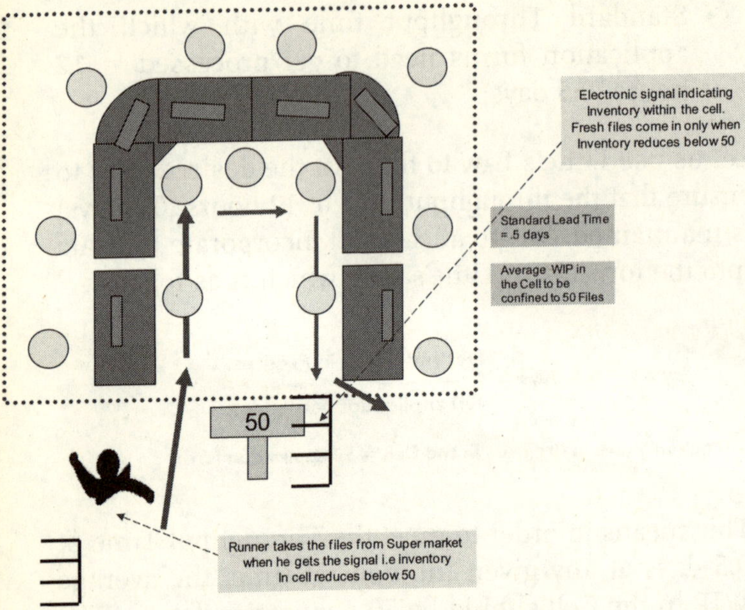

Fig 4.13: Stipulated Inventory in a Credit Processing Cell

Key Takeaways
■ In a Lean cell always maintain a standard inventory. ■ Little's Law can help you to create a pull system within a cell. ■ A pull system within a cell also requires a solid foundation of standard work procedures and multi-skilled employees. ■ In case the volumes go up, do not disturb the existing cell with pre-defined inventory. Create another cell with standard inventory.

Lesson 52

Being Aware of Wastes Can Make Business Acquisition Agile, Efficient and Effective

When you work on leaning your sales and marketing function, you should remember that there could be a hidden problem: burgeoning acquisition costs which you may not be aware of. Traditional accounting systems do not treat customers as acquired assets and costs associated with this get lost. Accounting systems being primitive, a large number of cost overheads may not be allocated in the right manner.

As I have always believed, the cost of customer acquisition is a key metric for sales and marketing performance. Tracking this metric can be a good indication of the health of Lean application in sales and marketing. Table 4.29 summarizes the 12 wastes which are associated with customer acquisition, as I have discovered during my leaning of sales and marketing functions/processes. Though meant for service businesses, these wastes are fairly universal in nature and can be used in all types of businesses.

Table 4.29: Deb's 12 Wastes of Customer Acquisition

S No.	Type of Wastes	What is it	Additional Details
1.	**Waste of product/ brand inundation**	This is a waste associated with launching products more than required.	This is often done with an objective to acquire additional customers, but often without keeping customer needs and requirements in mind. Mindless addition of products not only stresses the businesses but also breeds unwanted complexity
2.	**Waste of misaligned distribution channel**	This is the waste associated with not leveraging the right distribution channel for the targeted customer segment.	The distribution of products and service has to be done in a cost-effective manner by leveraging the right channels. The focus should be to improve acquisition efficiency, meet the specific needs of the customers and achieve better penetration. For example, a bank may need to use low-cost channels such as the internet to target un-banked segments.
3.	**Waste of atrophied skills**	This is a waste associated with employees not continuing to have the desired skills to serve the customers.	This happens when sales colleagues are not adequately trained in a regular manner and lack the fundamental skills to manage long-term relationships.
4.	**Waste of hazy customer cohorts**	This is the waste associated with not unfurling the unique needs and requirements of customers within existing customer segments.	Within customer segments there could be specialized customer groups to whom organizations need to cater. For example, in the financial services domain, a mass-affluent segment could have unique customer groups such as retirees, investors, baby-boomers etc.

Table 4.28: Deb's 12 Wastes of Customer Acquisition (*continued*)

S No.	Type of Wastes	What is it	Additional Details
5.	**Waste of customer ownership**	This is a waste associated with inadequate ownership of the total customer relationship.	In many companies, the customer is handled by a large number of functions because of which no one really owns the customer. The ownership of the customer gets passed on from one function to another. For example, in a cell phone service provider, the customer gets acquired by the sales team, after which the details are passed on to the customer service teams for ongoing issues. These customer service employees just address the service issues and there is nobody to manage the customer relationship.
6.	**Waste of inadequate existing customer focus**	This is the waste associated with not leveraging the existing customer relationship for furthering business.	This happens when companies do not focus on acquiring the wallet-share of existing customers. Or even if there is a focus, the current process of cross-sell is not effective. For example, a bank should offer products at various life events of the customer.
7.	**Waste of coordination**	This is the waste associated with follow-ups and back and forth actions which occurs in the acquisition process.	These are typically associated with efforts spent on cross-functional coordination.

Table 4.28: Deb's 12 Wastes of Customer Acquisition (*continued*)

S No.	Type of Wastes	What is it	Additional Details
8.	**Waste of dissonant partnership**	This is the waste associated with not leveraging the potential partners or entities beyond the company, to further business.	This happens when organizations do not thread relationships with partners to gather and serve the customers better and profitably.
9.	**Waste of inflexibility**	This is the waste associated with a firm's inability to embed flexibility into its products or services.	This waste can be avoided when flexibility is built into product design to allow the creation of products at short times. This can be achieved when organizations modularize product components so that new products and features can be assembled based on the changing demands of the customer.
10.	**Waste of wrong selling**	This is a waste associated with selling the wrong product to the customer.	This happens when the focus of the organization is not on providing profitable solutions to the customer but on somehow selling whatever is available.
11.	**Waste of missed opportunities**	This is the waste associated with being not able to fathom the emerging opportunities.	This happens when the company is not able to proactively sense and respond to the changing needs of customers, competitive pressures and market dynamics. This requires creation of capability within the firm to meet precise customer demands amidst changing market conditions. Also, organizations need to identify growth opportunities for newer products or services.

Table 4.28: Deb's 12 Wastes of Customer Acquisition (*continued*)

S No.	Type of Wastes	What is it	Additional Details
12.	**Waste of missing processes**	This is a waste due to lack of processes within the sales and marketing function.	To address this problem, organizations need to treat business acquisition as a process and embed it with a large number of metrics to track its performance on an ongoing basis.

One may ask how these are different from the eight wastes of Toyota which we have discussed in Lesson 38. Well, those wastes are quite universal but having specific wastes around customer acquisition helps sales and marketing colleagues to relate better. Otherwise, the debate can always be that Toyota's eight wastes are not applicable in sales and marketing functions. Identifying the wastes around customer-acquisition can be of great help. Learning not to see them will only add to customer acquisition costs.

Identifying the wastes in business acquisition is the first step towards making them Lean. This may appear to be a tall order as the sales and marketing functions are traditionally thought to be not amenable to process thinking. Also, the general belief is that friends from sales and marketing are too busy getting business and not bothered about the hidden in-efficiencies. This is quite an incorrect view.

If you are able to show the sales colleagues the hidden wastes in their processes, they would be the first people to adopt them, as it helps not only make their processes efficient but also meet customer demands, and that too in a cost-effective manner. The intervention of Lean should help to focus the company around profitable customers and building a profitable relationship.

So where does one begin and what are the few things that an organization should do to instill Lean thinking in sales and marketing processes?

Here is a list of Do's which you may like to look at to build a Lean customer acquisition process:

- Train all sales and marketing colleagues on the 12 wastes of customer acquisition.
- Do the value-stream mapping of all sales and marketing processes to uncover hidden wastes.
- Create flexible platforms with modularized components to generate new products at short notice.
- Build an engine within the company to sense and respond to changing customer demands.
- Leverage potential partners to serve the customer in a cost-effective manner.
- Scan existing market segments to find out the customer cohorts within them.
- Align channels with products to facilitate revenue maximization in a cost-efficient manner
- Pinpoint the unmet needs of the customer.
- Ensure that business acquisition professionals have adequate weightage to acquire new customers and increase the wallet-share of existing customers.
- Focus on a mutually beneficial relationship.
- Focus on the life-time value of customer relationship.
- Use analytics to target appropriate customers.

- Optimize existing processes.
- Track the following metrics:
  - Trend of overall acquisition costs,
  - Channel wise acquisition costs,
  - ROI of marketing costs,
  - Market share,
  - Rate of customer acquisition,
  - Life time value of customer.
- Clearly enunciate when to draw a line with customers – all relationships are not profitable.

Remember, Lean thinking is not about acquiring a large number of customers but focusing on profitable customers.

Key Takeaways
■ Leaning of the sales and marketing function is about aligning acquisition economics with customer economics. ■ Customer acquisition processes are often mired with wastes which we need to identify. ■ Deb's 12 Wastes of Customer Acquisition helps to see the unseen wastes – train all your sales colleagues on them. ■ Align the right channels with your sales processes to get the desired results.

FROM THE TRENCHES: Leverage the power of *Kaikaku* or Lean Breakthroughs

I was instrumental in introducing Lean Breakthroughs to the service sector in Asia during the early 2000s. Today, a large number of service companies have been following this model for rapid improvement.

So what is Kaikaku? The word Kaikaku means instant revolution in Japanese. Also, emanating from the Toyota stable, manufacturing companies have been using it successfully over the last decade. Also called Lean Breakthrough or Kaizen Blitz or Lean Event, Kaikaku aims at a spectacular improvement in a short period of time in a focused area using a dedicated team. Remember, if the results are less than spectacular it is not a Kaikaku. Popularized by individuals such as Masaki Imai, James Womack and the Association of Manufacturing Excellence in the US, Kaikaku is about just not planning but acting on problems now. It is about 'learning by doing'. A Kaikaku happens with the involvement of an empowered set of individuals who can take any decisions pertaining to the change.

Putting together an appropriate team is critical to the success of Kaikaku. Typically the team size should be anywhere from six to ten individuals. The composition should be mix of individuals from the work area impacted by the Kaikaku, outside the department and customers/suppliers. It is important to have individuals with lots of new ideas and having a can-do attitude.

(*Continued*)

Select an individual with good facilitation skills and participatory management. For a services business, it is important to have representatives from departments such as information technology, compliance, finance and legal. However, if they are not available for a full time basis they could be on call as and when required.

A Kaikaku begins with a training session to team members who implement all that they have learnt on resolving the problem within five days. Table 4.30 is a typical schedule for a Lean Breakthrough for a services business.

Table 4.30: Schedule for a Typical Lean Breakthrough in a Service Setup

Days of the Week	Details
Monday	Basic training, Align objectives, Tour the work area, Process walk, Time observation, Data analysis
Tuesday	Waste identification, Value-stream mapping, Spaghetti diagram, Process base lining (lead time, defects/errors, first pass yield, customer service, productivity, process efficiency), Tact time calculation
Wednesday	Improvement opportunities, Root cause identification, Manpower numbers (actual versus new), New process and layout design, Alignment with all stakeholders, Competency mapping, Process manual, Role redefinition, Load balancing
Thursday	Training of associates, New process roll out, Implement countermeasures, Install new measurements, 5S
Friday	New process up and running, Training complete, SOPs functional, Comparison as-is/to-be metrics, Action plan for next 30 days, Wrap-up presentation to leadership, celebration

(*Continued*)

Sometimes it is fine to extend the duration by a day or two. But the closure of project should immediately be followed by a presentation of results to the business leader/project sponsor by the team.

My team and I are credited with catalyzing more than 350 Lean breakthroughs in a services context. Such projects have delivered phenomenal improvements in the domain of productivity, lead time, distance traveled, hand-offs etc.

Sources: Sarkar, Debashis, *Lean for Service Organizations and Offices: A Holistic Approach for Achieving Operational Excellence*, ASQ Press, Milwaukee; 2008.

Sarkar Debashis, 'Kaikaku: The Improvement Blitzkrieg', *The Smart Manager*, Vol 5, Issue 4, Jun-Jul 06, Mumbai, India.

Lesson 53

Mindless Standardization of Processes does not Work in Services

Companies embarking on a Lean adoption go ahead and initiate enterprise-wide roll outs of standard processes. Practitioners of Lean often get standard-work (jargon for standardized procedure) done for all work that happens in the firm. You will see such procedures being displayed across the desks of associates doing jobs such as data entry, customer service, billing, hospital surgical preparations, account relationship management, design etc. This is done usually because of a senior level dictate and is not something which would enable their work. Have we not seen those colourful standard works on desks, looking very attractive but rarely used? Why does this happen?

This happens because the person who is providing thought leadership around Lean has not fully understood where the principles of standardization are relevant. Because Lean talks about standard-work, all processes are documented in detail with a belief that this will help. This approach is very myopic in nature. We should never forget that the outcome of Lean is to make a positive impact on customers and not just on standardization. So, it is imperative to understand where the principles of standardization can have a positive impact on customer experience. The other day I attended a conference wherein the global quality leader of a leading service company said that they had standardized all their processes irrespective of the functions and context. When I asked him the impact of this on customer experience, he dodged my question and did not respond. The response did not surprise me.

Does this mean that in a service context processes should not be standardized? Is it true that standardization generates waste in service processes?

Standardization is required but cannot be carried out in a mindless manner. Standardization in service businesses should be done based on the context and the type of process that has been taken up for improvement. For example in a retail bank branch, the DD (demand-draft) or cash process can be standardized as this process is repetitive in nature. However, you cannot standardize a process that handles queries. This is because queries vary widely and cannot all be addressed in the same way. Wherever you have processes that handle exceptions instead of standard queries, the teams should come up with a broad set of guidelines which customer-service executives can use. Standardization does not mean here that the customer services executives will become robots. Each of these processes (whether standardized or not) will have to be backed up by highly competent and empowered customer-services executives who are able to manage the interaction experience of customers.

Of course, standardization will result in waste when you try it on a process that does not require standardization. There are two approaches which can help you to make a decision on whether standardization is the right strategy for you.

Approach 1

Remember that there are two things that drive standardization: **Visibility** and **Variability** in Customer Requirement. Visible processes are those wherein the customer is involved and the process acts on them. In a non-visible process the information and material provided by the customer is worked on. In the former, quick response times and customer-interaction skills are critical, while in the latter there is a lag between customer request and delivery. The higher the visibility of a process, the greater the degree of variability in customer requirements, and hence, the greater the requirement for customization. Processes which require a higher degree of customization should not be standardized while the ones which happen behind the scenes can be standardized. Figure 4.12 summarizes this concept. I would recommend that before embarking on a Lean transformation, all processes should be placed on a scale like the one shown here, and then you can make the decision to standardize or not standardize these processes.

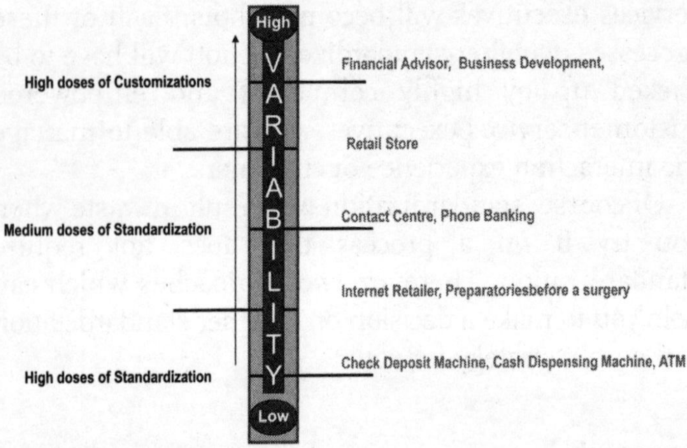

Fig 4.14: Process Visibility and Degree of Standardization

Approach 2

This is the better approach to decide whether to standardize a process or not. I would recommend that we use Hall and Johnson's approach.

Joseph M. Hall and M. Eric Johnson have come up with a matrix (Figure 4.13) which tells you which processes should be standardized and which should not be.

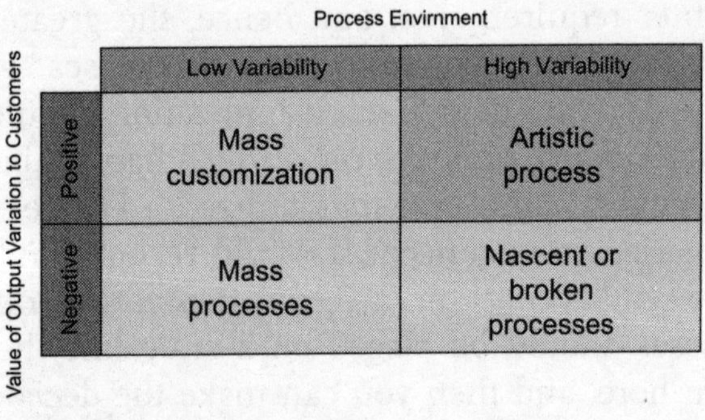

Fig 4.15: The Process Matrix

In this process matrix, what is shown on the y-axis is the value of service/product output variation to the customer. The x-axis shows the degree of variability in the inputs of the process. Looking at variability of output and input of a process, there are four types of process before us. Let us look at each of them in detail as researched by Hall and Johnson:

Mass processes: These are processes which require low variability in process input and output. Here the customer is looking for standard products or services for a narrow range of product or services. The focus should be to create standard processes which facilitate achieving these objectives. The examples where such processes are required are: automobiles, steel, aluminium, consumer durables, consumer financial products etc.

Mass customization: There are processes wherein there is low variability of product input and the customer values variability in the process output. Here standard processes are required to produce controlled variation in product or service output. The best example in this category is Dell's personal computers which cater to the unique requirements of customers.

Nascent or broken processes: These are processes wherein input variability to the process is high and the process cannot create the consistent output that the customer demands. These are those processes that use new materials, design or technology. Typically these processes, being newborn, have yet to mature. The approach to deal with such processes could be either of the following:

- Since the output variability is high, see if customers can appreciate it. If they do, treat them as an artistic process,
- If customers do not tolerate variation, focus should be on arresting the variation and creating standard process for the same.

Artistic processes: These are processes which have a high variability in input as well as output. Here the customer values the variability in product or services that is being provided to them. Also, the inputs that trigger the process vary, making it challenging for the company. In such a case, focusing on reducing variation by standardizing the process is a wrong approach. The endeavour should be to provide a set of guidelines that allows the exercise of judgment and also the ability to improvise the processes based on the context.

In a hotel, the guests come up with wide array of requirements. In such a case, providing employees with standard-work is not the right thing to do. Providing them standard script such as: '*Look into customers' eyes, Say 'Good Morning/Good Afternoon/ Good Evening,' Use words such as 'certainly' , 'it's my pleasure*', may not be fully effective. This is because each customer contact is unique and would require unique responses. Instead, providing them with directional guidelines can be more helpful. This could include statements such as: *I will build an engaging relationship with customers, I will look at each customer contact to delight the customer, I will ensure that the customer's stay at the hotel becomes memorable.* An approach like this ensures that the unique needs of customers are taken care of and the responses based on what the customer wants.

Other examples of artistic processes wherein standardization should not be done but only guidelines should be provided are:

- Customer contact centre,
- Writing code for a new software development,
- Relationship management with wealthy customers,
- Business development,
- Auditing,
- Customer service,
- Leadership training.

In the context of Lean application to service business, understand the complexion of the process in the Process Matrix (Figure 4.13) and accordingly take a decision.

To summarize, do not mindlessly standardize all service processes. Look at the context and take decisions.

Key Takeaways
■ Do not mindlessly standardize all processes in service organizations. ■ Understanding the variability of process input and output is a key before we embark on standardization. ■ Artistic processes should not be standardized but enabled with guidelines.

Epilogue

I hope you have enjoyed reading the lessons. It would make me happy if you are able to apply some of the learnings in your business. The learnings are fairly universal in nature and can be applied in services companies across industries such as aviation, manufacturing, health-care, government, hospitality, energy etc. However, the adoption is not going to be easy. If you look at it from the service perspective, the following are the challenges which I see coming in your way:

Leadership Commitment

If Lean thinking has to really take shape in services, leaders need to drive it. There are not too many CEOs who have really bought into this concept. I think this is where thought leaders on Lean management have to play a role in making them aware of its power. For leaders who say that this is a manufacturing concept and may not be applicable to services, share with them the examples of successful implementations. While we still do not have a service organisation which has embedded Lean thinking as a culture, we do see a few early successes. I am quite confident that out of this morass a successful role model organization will emerge which the world will look up to.

Culture

Change leaders need to remember that the culture of Lean thinking grows organically. There is no magic wand to get results. The culture of the organization will only change over a period of time when leaders take the organization with them and relentlessly drive it. It's when the impact is made on the visible and non-visible aspects of culture that we start seeing the change. Of course, it has to be backed with persistence, discipline and relentless communication.

Yet Another Methodology

Unfortunately Lean is being viewed as another of those rattles from the bags of practitioners who keep the company's engagement on improvements. When you see the improvement group propagating Lean as a methodology, you can at the most see a few successful projects. To make it an enterprise-wide phenomenon it has to be driven by the CEO and his direct reports. The improvement teams can introduce this concept to the top management of the company and share with them what it can do. Remember, to get the full power of Lean, leverage it as a way of doing business.

Long Term versus Short Term

Sometimes performance improvement approaches like Lean are looked as another method for short-term gains. While there is nothing wrong in this, it is important to keep in mind the impact that Lean management will have in the next 5, 10, 15 and 20 years. My suggestion is that if you are keen on doing what Toyota did to drive operational excellence, you have to be at it for the long haul. When you have a long term view of Lean management and are at it for many years, you will realize how positively the fabric of the company changes.

Sustaining enthusiasm

Sustaining the enthusiasm of the organization is critical in a Lean journey. Or else, you will see that enthusiasm is high when quick results set in, especially after the success of Lean breakthrough projects. However, later on, you may see the attention of the employees fading. This is where it is important that leaders need to pull back the energy of the employees if they see it fading out. While sharing the organizational vision of the company, leaders need to share how Lean management will help them in achieving it. This is where an exercises done through *Hoshin Kanri* (policy-deployment) will help them to know their contribution in this journey.

I do not want to end the book on a note of pessimism. I am also not trying to say that all these challenges are unsurmountable. But as a change leader it may be of help if you get to know the possible roadblocks so that you can plan your strategy accordingly.

Yes, this is not an easy task, like all change agenda. But, as Niccolo Machiavelli said:

> *There is nothing more difficult to take in hand, more perilous to conduct, or more uncertain in its success, than to take the lead in the introduction of a new order of things.*

Glossary

5S: 5S is a Japanese approach to workplace organization. Successful deployment of 5S leads to enhancing workplace efficiency, team productivity and employee engagement. A key metric of 5S is document retrieval time.

Anchors: Anchors are the building blocks that support the architecture of a Lean management system. The anchors comprise people, processes, partners, problem-solving and promotions.

Business-Value-Added Time: This is the time spent on business-value-added steps in a process.

Cell: This also referred as cellular-layout which is an all-encompassing operating unit that has all the activities of a process placed sequentially next to each other with the objective of producing a product or service, in the shortest possible time, and with minimum errors.

Chief Improvement Officer: S/he is the person responsible for catalyzing Lean transformation in the company. S/he may also be known as a Lean Leader, Lean *Sensei*, Head–Lean Deployment, Head–Organizational Excellence etc.

Consumer: This refers to the person or entity who finally uses or consumes the product or service produced by a company.

Customer: The next team or person in a process who is the recipient of the item/s produced by a team/ individual. This is a part of a larger process to manufacture of goods or service. Sometimes the word customer also denotes the person or entity who finally consumes the goods or service.

Cycle Time: This is the time taken to execute a task in a process. This helps to measure the time taken to complete the smallest unit of work in a process.

DEB-LOREX™ Model: This is a management system for achieving organizational excellence using the principles of Lean. Targeted towards service companies, the model has universal application. DEB-LOREX™ is an acronym for *Deb's Lean Organizational Excellence Model.*

DMAIC: This refers to steps used for solving a problem using a Six Sigma methodology. DMAIC stands for Define, Measure, Analyze, Improve, Control.

Efficiency: The efficiency of a process is defined as its ability to operate within given resources.

Effectiveness: The effectiveness of a process is defined as its ability to meet the requirements of the customer.

First-Pass Yield: This is the percentage of the product or service that leaves the process without defects and without having to be reworked.

Ground Zero Walk: Leaders walking around the offices and workplaces to get a feel for what is happening.

Kaizen: This is a Japanese word which means change for better

Lead Time: This is the end-to-end time required for the execution of a process which starts from the time the customer places the order and ends when the customer receives the product or service.

Lean Breakthrough: This refers to a spectacular and rapid improvement in a focus area carried out in a short period of time. It is also called a Kaizen Event, a Kaikaku, a Kaizen Breakthrough or Lean Event.

Lean Office: A team which is entrusted with catalyzing lean thinking in the company. A Lean Office houses experts on Lean methodology.

Lean Maven: These are individuals who are adept in the science of Lean operations.

Little's Law: This is a fundamental principle of operations management which states that the average number of works-in-progress in a stable system is equal to the completion rate multiplied by their average time in the system.

Ostrich Syndrome: This refers to a state in a workplace when the people working there are not aware of the hidden inefficiencies/wastes present there.

Problem: The gap between a current state and a desired state.

Procedure: This refers to the method of doing work in a process.

Process: A set of activities that work in tandem to produce a specific product or service for a customer.

Process Efficiency: Also called Value-Added Ratio, this is the ratio of value-added time spent in a process in relation to the total lead time.

Process Loop: This refers to the end-to-end processes which operate within a value stream. Examples of process loops are processes such as order-to-cash, application-to-disbursement, concept-to-launch etc.

Process Owner: These are individuals who own process loops or end-to-end processes and have authority to change them.

Pull: This means producing a product or service only when the customer demands it.

Push: This means producing a product, storing the same as inventory and then trying to sell it to the customer.

Service: This is activity carried out to meet the specific requirements of a customer.

Standard Process: This refers to a best known method of doing work. A standard process is achieved with the combination of optimized work content and desired skills.

Support Process: These are processes that support the value-creating and value-enabling processes of an organization. Typically, they are similar across the organization and cut across functional silos and strategic business units.

System: A set of components working towards the achieving of a larger whole.

***Takt* Time:** The German word takt means rhythm of music. Takt time determines how fast a process needs to run to meet customer demand.

Task: This is the smallest unit of work. Sometimes the word 'activity' is used synonymously with 'task' but more accurately, a set of tasks form an activity, while a set of activities form a process.

Throughput Time: This is the time taken in the execution in a process. It is the time taken to complete a process from start to finish. This is also called Door-to-Door time.

Value-Added Time: This is the time spent in doing value-added activities in a process.

Value-Creating Process: These are processes that directly (a) help in achievement of strategic business objectives, (b) contribute to customer satisfaction, and (c) facilitate output delivery.

Value-Enabling Process: These are processes that work closely with value-creating processes but do not directly impact business results, customer satisfaction and output delivery.

Value Stream: All activities in a business that are required to be done to bring a product from concept to launch and from order to delivery. A generic value stream comprises elements such as new product development, customer acquisition, order administration, order fulfillment, customer service and collections.

Value-Stream Mapping: A tool for identifying wastes in processes. An output of the value-stream mapping is a value-stream map.

Value-Stream Owner: This is the person responsible for an entire value stream and has total accountability for the overall performance (including profit and loss) of the product/product family that the value stream covers.

References

Chase, R. B. and Stewart, D. M. 'Make Your Service Fail-safe.' *Sloan Management Review,* Spring 1994 (Volume 35, Number 3), 35.

Guarraia, Peter and Andrew Schwedel, 'For Banks in Need – Getting more from Lean Six Sigma', Paper published by Bain and Company, Aug 26, 2008, New York.

Gerstner. Louis V, *Who Says Elephants Can't Dance?: Leading a Great Enterprise through Dramatic Change,* Collins Business, Nov 2002.

Graban, Mark, *Lean Hospitals: Improving Quality, Patient Safety and Employee Satisfaction,* CRC Press, Boca Raton; 2009.

Hall, Joseph M and M Eric Johnson, 'When Should a Process be Art, Not Science', *Harvard Business Review,* March 2009.

Konz, Stephen. *Facility Design*. John Wiley and Sons, New York: 1985.

Liker, Jeffrey K, *Toyota Way*, New York: McGraw Hill, New York: 2004.

Liker, Jeffrey K. and Michael Hoseus, *Toyota Culture: The Heart and Soul of the Toyota Way*, McGraw Hill, New York: 2008.

Osono, Emi.; Norihiko Shimizu, Hirotaka Takeuchi, *Extreme Toyota: Radical Contradictions That Drive Success at the World's Best Manufacturer*, John Wiley & Sons Inc, Hoboken, New Jersey: 2008.

Rummler, Geary A.; Alan P. Brache (1995). *Improving Performance: How to Manage the White Space in the Organization Chart*, Jossey Bass Business and Management Series. Jossey-Bass.

Sarkar, Debashis, 'Customer Guarantees', *The Smart Manager*, Aug-Sep 05, Vol 4, Issue 5, Mumbai, India

Sarkar, Debashis, 'Kaikaku – The Improvement Blitzkrieg', *The Smart Manager*, Vol 5, Issue 4, Jun-Jul 06, Mumbai, India.

Sarkar, Debashis, *5S for Service Organizations and Offices: A Lean Look at Improvements*, ASQ Press, Milwaukee: 2006.

Sarkar, Debashis, *Lean for Service Organizations and Offices: A Holistic Approach for Achieving Operational Excellence*, ASQ Press, Milwaukee: 2008.

Schein, Edgar, 'Coming to a new awareness of organizational culture', *Sloan Management Review*, 1984, Vol 25, No, 2, pp 3–16.

Shiba, Shoji and David Walden, *Breakthrough Management*, CII, New Delhi: 2006.

Smith, Gerald F. *Quality Problem Solving*, Prentice Hall India, New Delhi: 2000.

Sobek, Durward K, and Art Smalley, *Understanding A3 Thinking: A Critical Component of Toyota's PDCA Management System*, Productivity Press, Boca Raton, FL: 2008.

Swank, Cynthia Karen, 'The Lean Service Machine', *Harvard Business Review*, Boston: Oct 2003.

Womack, James P, and Daniel T Jones, *Lean Solutions – How Companies and Customers Can Create Value and Wealth Together*, Free Press, New York: 2005.

http://www.usatoday.com/money/workplace/2007-08-12-no-manage_N.htm

http://www.autofieldguide.com/articles/010502.html

http://www.dau.mil/educdept/mm_dept_resources/navbar/Lean/intro.asp

http://www.signetconsulting.com/methods_stories/proven_methods/after_action_reviews.php

http://www.mvr.usace.army.mil/PublicAffairsOffice/2003AnnualReport/DistrictHighlights/AfterActionReviews.htm

http://www.inc.com/resources/office/articles/20051201/morgan.html\

http://www.businessweek.com/managing/content/mar2009/ca2009036_859937.htm

http://www.bain.com/bainweb/PDFs/cms/Public/FINAL-Lean%20Six%20Sigma-Financial%

INDEX

5S, 26, 69–70, 76–77, 263
A3 thinking, 154–55, 220
abnormality, identification of, 46, 80, 82, 240
activities, business, 5, 34
  non-value-added, 4, 14, 15, 16, 20, 195
  value-added, 14–15, 16, 20, 195, 196
activity-based costing, 20
after action reviews (AAR), 166
analysis, 27, 49, 98, 155, 156, 159 ,192, 198, 209, 221, 236, 263
Armour, Stephanie, 108
  'Who Wants to be a Middle Manager?', 108
artifacts of culture, 64
attrition, 89–91, 232
  arresting, 91–92

benefits of A3 thinking, 156, 160
best-practice sharing, 150
Brache, Alan P., 203
business, activity, 5
  objectives, 35, 42, 53, 72, 128, 152, 206, 207, 235
    strategic, 125, 130, 206–07, 280
business-value-added activities, 14–15, 16, 20, 196, 197

capability-building, 145, 150, 199, 208
challenges, 10, 30, 33, 92, 205
  for middle management, 85–86, 108
  to Lean implementation, 20, 43, 64, 83, 85–86, 166, 176, 184, 271
command-control leadership style, 79, 80–81
company, goals of a, 9, 25, 55–56, 110
  manufacturing, 29, 122
  philosophy of a, 2, 9, 10, 61
  purpose of a, 2
  services, 4, 79, 126
consultants, role of, 26, 36
consumer, impact on the, 56, 95–96, 142, 248

cost efficiency and Lean, 18–22
costing, activity-based, 20
cross selling, 215–17, 224, 235, 257
  pull-based, 215–17, 234, 248
  push-based, 215, 233, 234, 235
cross training of employees, 208–12
culture, 64–65
customer guarantee, do's for, 56–58

delivery dissonances, 98
  corrections of, 98–100
Deming, William Edward, 219
Deming's wheel, 172, 219
DMAIC (Define-Measure-Analyse-Improve-Control), 221

employees, role of, 68, 86
  multi-skilling or cross-training of, 208–12
  treating, 90–91
enablers of management system , 116
evaluation, 5, 15, 20, 31, 75, 87, 97
excellence, 25, 26, 28, 55, 60–61, 143, 161, 203, 237, 274

Gerstner, L., *Who Says Elephants Can't Dance?*, 103
goals of a company, 9, 25, 55–56, 110

Hall, Joseph M., 268, 269
hansei, 165–66
holistic, approach, 4, 36–37, 76, 101, 117, 161, 164, 239
  repository, 140
Hoseus, Michael, 221

inventory in the service company, 126, 178, 181–82, 183, 193–99, 246, 253–54

Jefferson Pilot Insurance, 12
Johnson, M. Eric, 268
Jones, Daniel, 7–9

knowledge, 27, 62, 147, 149, 150, 160, 168, 176, 199
Krafcik, John, 7

large improvement projects (LIP), 41, 169–74
lead time, 5, 58, 77, 118–23, 126, 171, 238, 252, 254, 263–4, 278
  impact on quality, 126
leadership, 4, 21, 41, 44–45, 56, 66–69, 77, 86, 89, 97, 102–4, 107, 115, 116, 127, 135, 147, 228, 234, 260, 265, 268, 271
  command-control, 79, 80–81
Lean Alignment Teams (LATs), 74
Lean health assessment tool, 130–31
Lean implementation, challenges to, 20, 43, 64, 83, 85–86, 168, 181, 270
  positive impact of, 52–54, 61, 124, 128, 266
    cost/revenue, 125–26
    customers, 126, 266
    employees, 125
    flexibility, 125
Lean management process, 27, 112
  philosophy of, 2–4, 6, 24, 28, 62, 94,
  roadmap for implementation of, 41–43
Lean office, 36, 41, 145–46, 151–53, 222–23
  changing role of central, 149–52
  composition of, 145–46
  key roles in, 146–47
  focus on, best-practice sharing, 150
    capability-building, 145, 151, 199,
    tracking ongoing performance, 150,
Lean opportunity questionnaire, 187–89
Lean transformation, 2, 11, 12, 16, 35, 55, 62, 64, 81, 82, 85, 114, 115–16, 122–25, 128, 130, 138, 145–46, 163, 169, 180, 247, 251, 267,
  create interest in teams, 75
  preconditions for, 71–74, 78, 103–06
  structure of, 176

Lean, and cost efficiency, 18–22
  and urgency, 102–06
  challenges for adoption in services industry, 30–33, 85–86, 272–75
  definition of, 4
  eight wastes of, 175–79,
  misunderstanding of issues in, 24–28
  name selection of, 60–62
  relevance of, 109
Liker, Jeffrey, 8, 64, 176, 221
  & J. Shook, *Lean Thinking: Banish Wastes and Create Wealth in Your Corporation*, 8
  & M.Hoseus, *Toyota Culture: The Heart and Soul of the Toyota Way*, 221
  The Toyota Way, 9
LIP-SIP projects, 169–70, 174
Little, John, 243
Little's Law, 183, 243–47, 252–54

management process, Lean, 114
management system, enablers of, 117–18
  components of, 117
management, middle, 64, 68–69, 71–74, 78, 85–86, 107–10, 111, 170
    challenges for, 85–86, 108
  top, 57, 64, 66–69, 71–73, 77–78, 85, 98, 100, 108–09, 130, 134–35, 148, 170–71, 206, 208, 221, 222, 229, 273
Marchwinski, Chet & John Shook, *The Lean Lexicon*, 3, 137
measurement, system, 35–36, 38–39, 133, 209, 264
  metrics, 37, 38, 125, 209
    Deb's A to H principles of, 35–36, 39
    relevance of, 35, 38
MIS (Management Information Systems), 228
  reports, 187, 228–32
model, DEB-LOREXTM, 10–11, 116, 126, 127
multi-skilling, 209–13

non-value-added activities, 4, 14, 15, 16, 20, 196–97
norms of culture, 64–65

objectives, business, 35, 42, 53, 72, 124, 152, 206, 233
  strategic, 67, 125, 203–4,
observation, art of, 44, 49, 50, 192–200
  Deb's 10 rules for workplace, 46–49
  guideline for improving, 45–46
  objectives of, 45
office, Lean, 36, 41, 130, 147—53, 222–23
Ohno, Taichi, 165, 177
Osono, Emi et al, *Extreme Toyota: Radical Contradictions that Drive Success at the World's Best Manufacturer*, 103
ostrich syndrome, 177, 180

PDCA (Plan-Do-Check-Act), 154, 160, 165, 218–19
  problem solving steps, 155, 220–22
philosophy of, a company, 2, 9–10, 20, 61
  Lean management, 2–4, 6, 24, 28, 62
planning, strategic, 154, 155, 158, 160
Poka-Yoke, 26
positive impact of Lean implementation, 52–54, 61, 124, 127–28,
preconditions for Lean transformation efforts, 71–74, 78, 104–06
PRIDE, 143
problem reporting, 48, 82, 83
problem resolution & prevention, 220, 224
problem solving, 9, 64, 81, 92, 115, 154, 174, 220–24
  and A3 thinking, 154–57
  key facets of, 174
  key methodologies for, 26–28
process optimization, Deb's questionnaire on effectiveness of, 53–54

process ownership, 41, 46–47, 80, 132–36, 162, 204
approaches to drive, 133–35
lack of, 132–33
process thinking, beliefs to be instilled for, 21, 64, 94–96, 259
process, efficiency, 15, 80, 238
management system, 26, 163
mapping, 95, 96, 139–41, 143
metrics, 41, 128
mission / objectives, 14
repository, 141–45
processes, hierarchies of, 142–43
process-loops, 133, 139–41, 143, 210
projects, improvements of, 38, 86, 169
large improvement (LIP), 41, 169–70
LIP-SIP, 169, 170, 174
small improvement (SIP), 42, 169–70
proposal writing, 154, 159, 160
purpose of a company, 2

quiver approach, 24–26, 28, 87

redundancies, 32, 39, 177
duplication of functions/departments, 194, 198–201
irrelevant activities, 194–97, 200
overlapping of roles, 194, 195–98, 201
reflection, culture of, 10, 61, 158, 165–68
process, 165–68
relevance of, Lean, 109
Lean opportunity questionnaire (Deb's), 186–89
metrics, 35, 38
reports, 228–32
repository process, 99, 140, 142–43, 159
electronic, 141
physical form, 141
resistance, active, 84–85, 88, 103, 130
passive, 84–85, 88
role of employees at grassroots, 68, 85
Roos, Daniel, 7
Rummler, Geary A., 203

Sarkar, Debashis, 10, 40
self-service, 123, 190–93
service guarantee, 55–59
service intent, 98–101
service processes, 15, 30–33, 182, 183, 266
service recovery process, 224–27
services company, 4, 79, 123, 262
inventory in the, 122, 178, 181–85, 198–202, 244, 245–46, 253–54
Shewhart, Walter, 219
Shiba, Shoji, *Breakthrough Management*, 45
Shimizu, Norihiko, 103
Shook, John, 8, 137, 160
SIPOC-R, 31
Six Sigma, 26, 27, 29, 60, 62, 147
Smith, Gerald F., 45
standardization in service processes, 265–70
type of service processes, 267–70
visibility and variability in the process, 266–67
status reporting, 153
strategic planning, 153, 156, 157, 159
Swank, Cynthia Karen, 12

Takeuchi, Hirotaka, 103–04
targeting excellence, 25, 26, 28, 55, 60–61, 147, 161, 203, 237, 274–75
tasks, *see* activities
theory of constraints, 26
time, lead, 5, 58, 77, 118–23, 126, 171, 238, 252, 263–4
throughput, 5, 120–23, 243–45, 252
TINA, 103
Toyoda, Aiko, 104
tracking ongoing performance, 151, 212

treating employees, 90–91

value stream, 4, 8, 57, 61, 117, 133, 137–39, 141, 142, 145–47, 150–52
mapping of, 32, 37, 41–42, 76, 92, 95, 96, 260, 263
value-added activities, 14–15, 196
values, 65, 99, 214, 268–69
and underlying assumptions of the culture, 64–65
of activities, 16
visual board at workplace, 82–83, 142, 162, 240
visual management, 161–64, 237–42
tools, 164–65, 238

waste, awareness of, 41, 57, 109, 162, 182, 240
eliminate the, 31, 191, 194, 237
in service industry, 30–33, 263–64
of customer acquisition, 255–263
of Lean, 178–80
of measurement system, 35
of resources, 97–98, 228–29, 236
optimization, 180
reducing, 179, *see* redundancies, white spaces,
Watanabe, Katsuaki, 104
white spaces in the company, 203–05
WIP (work in progress), 243, 249–50
Womack, James P., 7, 8, 9, 176, 259